Of Primary Importance

Of Primary Importance

What's Essential in Teaching Young Writers

Stenhouse Publishers
Portland, Maine

Ann Marie Corgill

Foreword by JoAnn Portalupi

Stenhouse Publishers
www.stenhouse.com

Credits

Page 88: "The Whale" from *Beast Feast,* copyright © 1994 by Douglas Florian, reprinted with permission of Houghton Mifflin Harcourt Publishing Company.

Library of Congress Cataloging-in-Publication Data

Corgill, Ann Marie, 1971-
  Of primary importance : what's essential in teaching young writers / Ann Marie Corgill.
     p. cm.
  ISBN 978-1-57110-374-1 (alk. paper)
  1. English language--Composition and exercises--Study and teaching (Primary) I. Title.
  LB1528.C67 2008
  372.62'3--dc22
                          2008016719

Cover and interior design by Designboy Creative Group
Manufactured in the United States of America on acid-free, recycled paper
14 13 12 11 10 09 08   9 8 7 6 5 4 3 2 1

To my parents,
Gerald and Ann Corgill,
and to my dear friend Sharon Taberski,
with love and appreciation for
helping me grow in so many ways

Contents

Foreword

I first met Ann Marie Corgill in the fall of 1996, when I moved with my family to Birmingham, Alabama, and my son, Robert, was placed in her first-grade classroom. Robert was lucky to have her as a teacher not once but twice when, two years later, she moved to third grade and they were together again. Today, Robert is a graduating senior, ready to leave for college with dreams of writing professionally. Donald Graves said that all it takes is one great teacher to impact a child for life; Ann Marie Corgill was, for my son, that teacher. She offered Robert the tools and guidance to fully act as a writer and reader. Her belief in him—and in all of her students—was so strong that he couldn't help but believe in himself. Robert learned, during those early years, to see writing as a comfortable and joyful haven, a place he could return to on his own and with others throughout his years in school.

One might ask, "What happened in her classroom to incite a passion that could sustain itself over the years?" This book will show you that and much, much more.

Of Primary Importance introduces a teacher who knows her subject, understands her students, and isn't cowed by political pundits into turning away from her beliefs. Writing from the authority of her classroom, Ann Marie shows how her beliefs about teaching and learning affect everything she does in the classroom. She begins by discussing what she calls the "Six As" (analyze, ask, applaud, assist, assess, advocate) and, in doing so, offers a workable mantra that any teacher—new or veteran—can use to stay focused on the goal of developing strong writers.

Because Ann Marie believes that children can learn to speak as writers, she starts the year by listening to their words and then returns those words in ways that highlight their ability to do so. Because she knows that writing is a process of solving problems, she teaches her students to become problem-solvers. Because she values the learning path her students will take, she helps them to create "Writing Journey" folders that uncover for students—as well as for parents, friends, and herself—a rich view of their yearlong learning. Each big idea is embedded in the nitty-gritty details of the classroom: jammed staplers, dried-up markers, stories finished in two minutes flat. This continual shuttling between big idea and practical counterpart becomes the warp and weft of a book that ultimately invites readers to hone their own beliefs about teaching writing while it offers practical ways to work with children.

Ann Marie shows us that a teacher is also an architect, interior designer, environmental protection agent, and navigator—to name just a few of the varied roles we play. Her thoughtful teaching is expressed not only through her words, but also through her actions: how she designs space, organizes instruction, provides access to materials, and so forth. And, although readers quickly learn how much depends on the teacher in the classroom, we are constantly reminded of the important role the students themselves play in helping to create the learning community. In an era when external forces are guiding the hands of teachers, with little concern for the needs of specific students, it is refreshing to find a teacher who listens to her children's questions and statements to gather substance for the teaching points she will create for them.

Anyone who has spent a day in an elementary classroom knows the perils that lie within. *Of Primary Importance* is filled with reminders that all is not perfect. An oyster makes a pearl from a grit of sand. Likewise, Ann Marie creates skillful young writers out of sticky-handed, high-energy, not-always-eager-to-learn youngsters. She reminds us that a good teaching year is rich with student breakthroughs, but it also comes with false starts. There are exhilarating highs as well as moments of frustration. Her honesty is such that many readers will find in these pages their own messy classrooms. Her gift: filtering it through the lens of a teacher who embraces the messiness without losing the image of the skillful writers she is certain will emerge by year's end. And, by the steadfastness of her teaching, they certainly do.

A good book can be a mentor that points us toward a path while it brings out the best in us. At the heart of this book are detailed portraits of classroom studies on poetry, nonfiction, and fiction writing. While these chapters are solidly practical, Ann Marie delivers them with a belief that teaching is personal and idiosyncratic. She designs her words not to direct but to support the reader's own thinking and work in the teaching of writing.

For two years, Ann Marie was this parent's dream: a passionate, intelligent teacher who cared equally about her craft and her students. I am thrilled that others will have the chance to be touched by her light in the way that Robert, her students, and I were touched by her presence in our lives.

I believe that you will read *Of Primary Importance* and think more deeply about your teaching, feel more passionate about the possibilities, and be inspired by the beauty of what a new writing year with your students will bring.

JoAnn Portalupi

Acknowledgments

My heart is filled with appreciation for family, friends, colleagues, and students who have encouraged and supported my teaching and learning journey. Each one of you is a special part of my personal and professional "family tree," and I am grateful to all of you for your wisdom, your insight, your expertise, your generosity, your encouragement, your friendship, and your love.

- To my parents, Gerald and Ann Corgill, and my family for a lifetime of love and encouragement. Mom and Daddy, thank you for always being there to help me follow my dreams and for being proud of the work I do. Phala and Braden, Paul and Christine, thank you for cheering your sister on through all the times "Aunt Ree" couldn't join in on the fun but had to glue herself to the computer to write. To the Andrews and Corgill aunts, uncles, and cousins—and especially to Granny for reminding me to be myself and do what makes me happy.

- To Deanna Kimbrough—I first believed I was a reader and a writer because of your teaching.

- To Brenda Parker and Pam Pyron, for sharing your classrooms during my first student teaching experiences and for showing me firsthand what it means to be a responsive teacher.

- To Maryann Manning and Barbara Rountree, my graduate and undergraduate professors, for giving me a deep pedagogical understanding of best practice in literacy and for providing a firm foundation to stand on as I began my teaching career.

- To William Hagood and Toni Shay for years of generosity and friendship. You've supported my journey as a writer and learner in every way—shipping my entire library by UPS to New York City, dipping into the LexAmi inventory for the newest professional book to enhance my teaching, providing delicious dinners and networking opportunities too numerous to count, and giving me the opportunity to write and learn with Emily in Writer's Camp.

- To Kathy Snyder, my longtime friend and Riverchase colleague. I am deeply grateful for and inspired by your masterful teaching and mentoring, your organization (all those forms keep me together but freak me out!), and your optimism. I am a better person because of you, my dear friend.

- To Ralph Fletcher and JoAnn Portalupi for trusting me to teach your son Robert; for the weekly (and life-changing) visits to my first- and third-grade classrooms for writing workshop; and for sharing your knowledge and writing expertise. Your friendship means so much.

- To Shelley Harwayne for giving me the dream-come-true opportunity to teach at the Manhattan New School. Not only did you welcome me into the MNS family, you shared your beautiful home with this southern girl on her first trips to the Big Apple and made New York City feel like home from the very start. I am in awe of your brilliance and forever inspired by your deep commitment to always do what's right for children and teachers.

- To Sharon Taberski—words cannot express my thanks to you for the years of teaching, learning, laughing, shopping, and growing stronger with you as my friend. From soaking in your brilliant teaching as I sat on the pink rug in your classroom to those glorious New England Thanksgivings, I feel so lucky to have been "adopted" by you and your wonderful family. Thank you for being there no matter what as an amazing mentor and a forever friend.

- To the many professional writers, consultants, teachers, and researchers—those who've become friends and those whom I've never met. Your books on writing and reading are dog-eared on my nightstand, and your words resonate in my teaching every day. Thank you to Franki Sibberson, Karen Syzmusiak, Katie Ray, Lester Laminack, Reba Wadsworth, Regie Routman, Don Graves, Martha Horn, Lucy Calkins, Katherine Bomer, Linda Hoyt, Tony Stead, Cris Tovani, Stephanie Harvey, Debbie Miller, Dick Allington, and Jen Allen.

- To my esteemed colleagues at the Manhattan New School, Bronxville, Brookwood Forest, and Riverchase Elementary schools. This book has been inspired and encouraged by you, and I thank you all from the bottom of my heart. A special thanks to those incredible teachers who have also been incredible friends through this entire book-writing process (and who love me even when I don't answer the phone!): JoAnne Searle, Sharon Hill, Christina Murray, David Besancon, Felicia Weisberg, Kristi Lin, Angelika Kypar, Dianne Aronson, Kendall Fousak, Carla Rockhill, Sara Carpenter, Vickie Harris, Gayle Morrison, Annie Balestra, Blair Lynn, Elise Blackerby, Tracy Cole, Heather Brown, Jennifer Hendrix, and Jada LeCroy.

- To those MNS colleagues and friends who taught me so much and have now gone on to be principals, literacy consultants, and moms: Karen Ruzzo, Renay Sadis, Layne Hudes, Jacqui Getz, MaryAnne Sacco, Pat Werner, Sharon Hill, and Doreen Esposito—what lucky students and teachers to be under your leadership!

- To my fabulous first-grade team and Riverchase administrators, who immediately made me feel welcome and became my new school family. Thank you to Deborah Camp, Dianne Baggett, Alice Turney, Patti Tanner, Nichole Turner, Kinsley Hyche, Lisa Chick, and Ellen Hottel for your love and support and for willingly sharing your knowledge and teaching expertise with me. I am truly blessed to work with all of you.

■ To all the incredible people at Stenhouse, especially my editor, Bill Varner. Even when I didn't think I could write another sentence, you reminded me to "believe" and kept me going with the perfect suggestion, insightful idea, or encouraging email. Thank you for your patience and for waiting five long years for the birth of this book. I'd also like to thank Erin Trainer and Chris Downey for the on-target suggestions in those final stages of copyediting and for the hours and hours of production work that made this book come to life in such a beautiful way. To Jay Kilburn and Bill for designing such a gorgeous cover, one that will always remind me what's primarily important—the precious children we teach. To Doug Kolmar for your marketing expertise and to Philippa Stratton and Tom Seavey, who trusted that I had something important to say about teaching and writing years ago and gave me the time I needed to bring my thoughts and ideas to life.

■ Finally, to all the students (and their parents) I've been so fortunate to teach and learn alongside over the past fourteen years. Kids, it's your writing, your conversations, your publications, and your smart thinking that fill the pages of this book. Thank you for making my dream as a teacher of writing come true. Lots of love, a lifetime of thanks, and a big hug to all of you!

Introduction

Being a teacher changes your life. It changes your life because the minute you walk into that classroom, you're greeted by a room full of little people whose lives will be changed because of you. This book was born out of a commitment to support and make a difference in the lives of children and in writing instruction in today's classrooms. Several years ago, when this book wasn't even a clear vision (or a blip on the radar screen for that matter), I stopped to check my mail in the downstairs lobby of my apartment one day after school. In my mailbox was an encouragement letter, a "get-your-butt-in-the-chair-and-just-write" letter, along with a favorite quote from editor and friend Brenda Power. The quote inside the letter read: "Write the book you most desperately want to read."

I immediately knew that if I was choosing a new professional book to read that I would want a book that gave me a clear picture of the writing year in a primary classroom with unit of study overviews as well as teaching specifics. I can't teach without quality literature and am always on the lookout for great writing mentors for my students, so I knew I needed titles and book suggestions throughout this imaginary book I "most desperately" wanted to read. I love color photos and always revisit those books that contain pictures of classrooms, kids' writing, and management tools. I love knowing the inside scoop on where to buy cool materials and writing supplies and how to support kids in producing gorgeous published pieces of writing, so this had to fit somewhere in those yet-to-be-written chapters. I also wanted to read that life isn't perfect in first or second or third grade every day. Mistakes in planning and lessons that flop and writing that doesn't even look like writing are just as much a part of the success of the writing year as those magical writing moments. I wanted to read about real life in a classroom, because writing isn't the only thing we teach and writing isn't the only subject we have to wrap our brains around. Yes, we're striving to make this part of our day more productive and successful while at the same time we're

Perfecting a reading workshop and

Figuring out what the math is in the lesson we're teaching tomorrow and

Scheduling parent conferences and

Receipting field trip money and

Finding the bandage box to cover a freshly skinned knee and

Writing our weekly newsletter to parents and

Composing a thank-you card to the guest speaker who visited three weeks ago and

Finishing progress reports so they can be approved and sent home on Monday and

Remembering the monthly tornado drill is at 10:00 and we better not be outside at recess this time and

Wondering when the government will realize that the *No Child Left Behind* Act (NCLB) is leaving children behind right and left and

Just closing our door and making sure that the class of students in our care knows that they are the most important part of what we do each day.

This was the book I wanted to read, and this is the book I wrote.

I wrote it because I believe in teachers and children and quality writing instruction. Not in scripts. Not in top-down mandates. Not in cookie-cutter curriculum plans. Not in politicians and school officials who have never darkened the door of a classroom.

When I first moved to New York City, I would frequently stop the people who looked like serious New Yorkers to get directions. And more often than not, because I didn't have firsthand experience with the city streets and had no visual or background knowledge of landmarks, I usually got lost and ended up trying to flag down a taxi to take me back to my starting point. Those helpful New Yorkers just assumed that this southern girl simply needed step-by-step directions. That's all. But what I really needed was to pound the pavement myself, maybe making a wrong turn or taking the long way there, but not giving up because I couldn't follow the directions exactly. Professional books sometimes feel like step-by-step direction givers for teaching, showing you a "first this, then this, and finally this" way of classroom instruction. And more often than not, we end up lost and scrambling to get where we need to go by our own wits and experience. Teaching is not so simple as to be reduced to a recipe, a script, or a step-by-step direction. I want to make it clear that I strongly believe professional books are not Global Positioning Systems for teachers. I do not want you listening for the "Teach the lesson in one mile" and "Turn the page in 500 feet" voice in what I've written. It's important when reading this book to recognize that the goal is not to replicate what I've done (or what any author has done) but to use this information as support for your thinking and inspiration for your own original ideas. I believe that so much of what's happening in education today, so much of what's being published, is giving teachers permission not to think anymore. It is my hope and my sincere request that you think of this book as a friend standing by to cheer you on in your classroom. Use it as a resource to encourage your own thinking, support your own work, fill your head with questions and ideas, and energize you, not just as a teacher of writing, but most importantly, as a teacher of children.

I believe in you as a fellow teacher and in the children under your care and instruction. I believe it's essential for educators to remember that with a solid knowledge base, with sound curriculum plans, with developmentally appropriate expectations, and with core beliefs, *we* are at the heart of student success in writing and in every area of the curriculum.

If I could have my way, I'd take you by the hand and lead you into my primary classroom so you could see and hear and feel and be a part of the growth of young children into young writers. It is my sincere hope that this book will bring you vicariously into the workshop, into the writing conferences, into the reading and talking and writing and learning that happens over the course of a year in our classroom. I want to share my thinking and what I've discovered is essential in helping young writers grow. Join me for the planning, the "ah-ha!" teaching moments, the "what *was* I thinking?" moments, the reflections, the publications, the celebrations, and the realities of teaching writing in the classrooms of today. So come now, and be a part of our story.

Chapter 1
What's Essential in Teaching Young Writers?

> *Instruction begins when you, the teacher, learn from the learner;*
> *put yourself in his place so that you may understand…*
> *what he learns and the way he understands it.*
>
> —Søren Kierkegaard

Step inside and breathe the writing workshop air with me. Take a look at a primary classroom, and take a minute to watch and listen and see real learning, real writing in action.

Listen closely. Do you hear the voices? The room is filled with writing chatter: "I think I'm going to start my second page of my book!" "Where's that book we read this morning? I think it can give me some ideas for my illustrations." "I need a red crayon and a skin-colored one for my mom's face and lips!" "Have you had a conference with Miss Corgill today?" "I'm almost ready to start a new piece!" "How much longer till share time?"

Look closely. Do you see the work? We've got stories about monsters and bad guys that get married and live happily ever after, stories about summer vacations from the Poconos to Poland, and a bazillion "all-about-me" stories: My Dad and Me, My Mom and Me, My Cousin and Me, Me and My Friends, My Friends and I, I and My Friends, My Bird, My Dog, My Dinosaur. My Goodness! Lots of open folders, paper choices, "approximated" spellings, crayon-filled illustrations, and serious pencil grips. There are tables and rugs and corners and book nooks filled with little bodies, little people with big ideas about writing and bookmaking.

Can you feel the energy? It's an eager energy, a committed energy, an energy that radiates throughout the room and gives purpose to my teaching. It's an energy and an innocence that is far removed from test scores and writing prompts and worksheets and scripted curriculum guides. These students are eager and committed to their work because, like Katie Wood Ray and Lisa Cleaveland say in their book *About the Authors*, our writing workshop is also "a happy place where we make stuff" (2004, 1). That's the way writing should be. It is essential for young writers to have teachers who provide the following:

- Daily writing time
- Opportunities for writers to read the kinds of books they want to write
- Opportunities for choice in topic, format, or genre
- Demonstration, practice, teaching, and celebration during the workshop period
- Reasons to write for a purpose and an audience

- Support to the writer by using classroom library book authors and classmates as teachers in the classroom
- Tools necessary for writers to write and publish the kinds of pieces they envision
- Time for writers to think, talk, write, and share every day

Each morning for 180-plus days each year, we greet a group of students at the door of our classrooms. Some arrive well dressed and well fed and full of eagerness and energy for the day. Others arrive right after hearing their mom and dad's argument over breakfast. Some just barely saunter in because they stayed up until midnight watching cartoons. Some sigh with a breath of relief to be in a safe and happy place for the next seven hours.

Although we can't change a child's experiences outside the classroom, as professionals, we must strive to support these young writers and make a difference in their lives within the classroom. Through the years I've come to understand how my teaching practices, decisions, beliefs, and behaviors can directly affect the learning and success of young writers. In his article "What I've Learned About Effective Reading Instruction from a Decade of Studying Exemplary Elementary Classroom Teachers," Richard Allington speaks of six "Ts" of effective elementary literacy instruction: *tools, texts, teaching, trust, talk,* and *time.* In this article, Allington states, "It has become clearer that investing in effective teaching—whether in hiring decisions or professional development planning—is the most 'research-based' strategy available" (2002, 741).

This article and other works by highly regarded literacy experts have helped me clarify my own thoughts on the teaching of writing.

First things first. Teaching expertise matters. Who we are as teachers to our groups of students and writers matters more than any curriculum out there. Our students sink or swim because of us. So what kind of writing teachers do young children need?

Like Allington's Six Ts, I believe students succeed when their teachers possess what I call the Six As. The teachers who I believe are most successful in helping young writers grow strong are the ones who *Analyze, Ask, Applaud, Assist, Assess,* and *Advocate.*

ANALYZE

The Story of Rajah: The Fourth-Floor Window

Rajah was one of my thirty second graders—a writer, an artist, an inquisitive seven-year-old who proudly announced (every chance he got) that he had hair like Bob Marley and wanted to be an author when he grew up. At the beginning of the year, I learned that Rajah's mom had researched and found a school where Rajah could grow as a writer and a lover of literacy. She knew her child's passions, his strengths, and his needs as a learner and worked hard to find the perfect learning environment for him. I was honored that she had chosen our school for her son. That year Rajah and his family had moved from Seattle to New York City, and his mother, Rebecca, shared some amazing information with me at our first parent/teacher conference.

Rebecca began our meeting by walking across the room to the nonfiction area, to the window that faces the east side of the city. Rebecca wanted me to see that their apartment window was directly across from our classroom at Manhattan New School. She wanted me to know that she watched from that window (with binoculars, I might add) to see what her child was doing in school. Yikes! And I'm thinking to myself, *What* is this mother seeing? Is Rajah happy? Is he learning? Am I being the teacher she hoped and dreamed for her son when finding the perfect school in Manhattan?

Rajah and I have since moved from MNS, but his overly observant mother taught me a big lesson that day. She so clearly reminded me that analyzing—looking closely through our "teaching binoculars"—and learning about our students' passions, their strengths, and their needs as writers and as children isn't just a job for parents, it's for us, their teachers.

Children come with a wealth of knowledge and experience about their world and their lives in and out of the classroom. We need to learn *about* our students, learn *from* our students, and learn *with* our students if we want to teach writing well. Have you heard people say that when you're looking for something, many times it's right under your nose? Well, what I was looking for hit me right at the waist: the five-, six-, seven-, and eight-year-olds that were filling my classrooms year after year.

If we just watch and analyze how they work and interact in our classrooms each day, they will show us what they know and won't be afraid to tell us what they don't know. Get acquainted with your students and know them inside and out. Knowing your children is most important. Watch them. Learn from them. Create your lessons for them. Adjust your teaching because of them. It will change the way you think and act and teach if your children and their passions, their interests, their struggles, their lives are at the heart of your teaching.

ASK

The Story of Jahlil: The Mentor and the Met

Jahlil, one of my former second graders, who is now attending high school in New York City, comes to mind when I think of significant moments in my career as a teacher of writing. Because of situations beyond his control at home, Jahlil came to school late every morning and began the day frustrated and anxious. Looking through his writing folder (a tool I'll talk about in upcoming chapters), I found a newspaper clipping of a statue at the Metropolitan Museum of Art. (I had recently asked the children to collect artifacts that might help them tell their stories and support their writing work.) Having preconceived ideas about the experiences Jahlil had had in his life, I immediately discounted the clipping as nothing connected to his writing and just a way to fulfill a writing assignment. I didn't ask any questions. I just made assumptions.

Jahlil, like every child I have ever known, craved one-on-one time with his teacher, and one day, *he* asked for a writing conference. That day he confided in me about his life and his reasons for choosing that newspaper clipping. Jahlil said to me in response to one of my questions, "Ann Marie, I chose this clipping because it reminds me of my mentor, Jim. I don't have a dad, and Jim comes to my apartment every Tuesday to take me to do stuff. We go to the park. We go to museums. We take pictures and eat good snacks. This statue reminded me of one I had seen at a museum with Jim. I love Jim." And you can guess how I felt when Jahlil stopped talking. I felt like a teacher who deserved to just crawl under the table and die. I had labeled a child without knowing the full story. I had immediately made a decision that this child, because of his life and experiences, would have nothing to say in his writing. I had assumed that he wasn't doing the writing and thinking work that I expected of all the students. I didn't ask questions or talk to Jahlil before making these decisions or assumptions. But thanks to Jahlil, who did ask for that one-on-one time, thanks to that time I did listen to Jahlil's thinking and reasoning, thanks to a moment in my career where I was reminded of the importance of giving *all* children a chance to tell their stories, I was able to support Jahlil in being a writer with a purpose.

Jahlil wanted to thank Jim for all he had done, so with my help and the support of several mentor texts, Jahlil learned how to write a thank-you letter that day, and we mailed it to Jim the next week. This young writer had an audience, and he was writing with a clear purpose. Jahlil wanted to thank Jim that day. But I would like to give my heartfelt thanks to Jahlil for reminding me of what's of primary importance in teaching young writers: asking questions and listening first to the child. Ask children. Hear them. Teach children to ask the questions they want the answers to. Believe that what a seven-year-old has to say is important. Because it is. Just ask.

APPLAUD

The Story of Owen: The Crayon Crisis and the Rainbow Portal

On the first day of school this year, one of my new little first graders was doing everything but what I thought he should be doing in writing workshop. From my seat at the conference table, I watched as he skipped across the room and grabbed *every* crayon in the box at a table far from his workspace in the room. And as the other children at the table were yelling, "Owen took all the crayons!" this little guy simply ignored his classmates and began, with a two-handed grip, to scribble a giant circle of color onto his paper (with all twenty-four crayons, I might add). As soon as he finished his circle, he returned the crayons to their proper place, and the "He's not sharing! No fair! I need the red crayon, Owen!" ceased.

I called Owen to the conference table to meet with me so I could find out what this interesting paper full of colors might be. "Haven't you seen one of these before, Miss Corgill? It's a rainbow portal." As I looked at him, quite confused and quite shocked that a five-year-old was using the word *portal* in his explanation, Owen continued. "You know. A door that opens to an imaginary world." He then told the story of the creatures that lived behind this portal and the adventures they pursued. After our conference that day, Owen decided to add to that story and share it at our first publishing celebration of the year.

I have to be honest. It took all I had not to march myself over to the screaming table and intervene on the crayon crisis and ignore whatever Owen had written (or colored) on his piece of paper. But because I took a deep breath and took the time to confer about the purpose behind this madness, I was able to applaud the intentions of this young writer and celebrate where he was in his first-grade writing journey—rather than take the "stop-the-outrageous-behavior" route. Owen wasn't out to annoy his classmates by stealing all the crayons. He never thought once about not returning the materials to their proper place. And he never doubted that his work that day wasn't important writing work. Even if it's a big page of "crayon scribble," applaud the child for taking the risk, take him where he is as a writer, and begin to support and assist him in this yearlong writing journey.

ASSIST

The Story of Andre: From Korea to New York City

Andre came to Manhattan New School, to my second-grade class, from Korea. On the first day of school, his mom introduced him as tears were streaming down his sweet, chubby cheeks. Andre didn't speak a word of English, and Andre was afraid—so afraid that he gripped my hand, holding it as tightly as he could as we walked those three flights of stairs to Room 304. As the days turned into weeks and weeks turned into months, Andre began to make friends, Andre began to speak English, and Andre began to write. I learned that he loved *Star Wars*, Tom and Jerry, the second-grade bird study, and Rosemary Wells. He hated the 8:20 arrival time and entered the classroom bundled and sleepy eyed on those winter mornings, but he loved the warmer temperatures and throwing the football in the climbing yard with his friends Daniel and Scott. Watching Andre throw that football

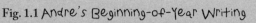

and learning alongside him that year made me think that sometimes school is like an NFL for children, with teachers as coach, cheerleader, referee, teammate, and fan all at once. And it's ultimately your assistance and your work with these little people that determines whether it's a winning season or not.

Throughout the year, I sat alongside Andre to assist him in daily class time and to allow him to have opportunities to hear the model of a fluent reader. He was exposed to multiple genres through read-aloud and writing workshop time and had daily talk time with friends. Because Andre wrote with the class every day, talked with friends and with me every day, and had multiple experiences with reading, writing, talking, and playing over the year, he wrote, and he proudly went to third grade as the author of poetry, fiction, procedural, persuasive, and informational texts. (See Figures 1.1 and 1.2 to see his growth as a writer.) At the end of that year, I realized that daily time and commitment to assist and support Andre was the best way to help him grow as a writer, reader, and speaker. With the appropriate tools, texts, and teaching, and a little assistance and support from his teacher and friends, Andre was given what he needed to learn the English language; to learn how to express his thinking, his ideas, his knowledge, and his passions; and to become the writer he was meant to be.

Fig. 1.1 Andre's Beginning-of-Year Writing

Fig. 1.2 Andre's End-of-Year Writing

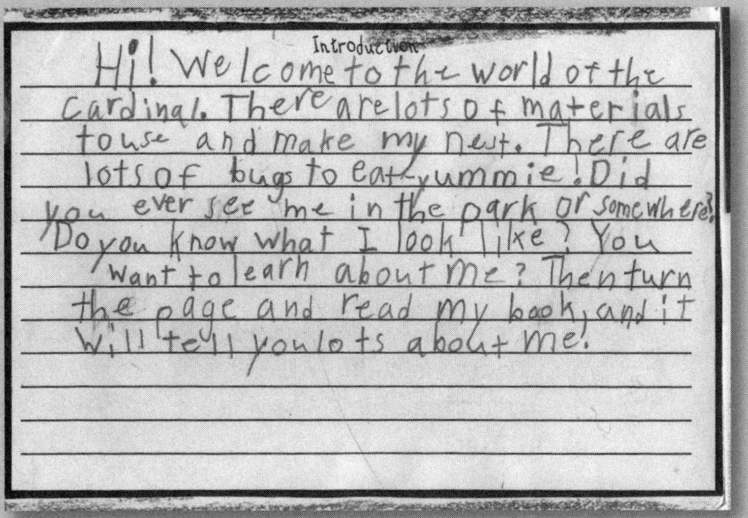

ASSESS

The Story of Robby: The "Out-of-the-Bubble" Thinker

Last year I worked in a school district in suburban New York that required first graders to take an end-of-year standardized literacy test. I'll never forget those two days in May when my six- and seven-year-old students were required, with #2 pencils in hand, to complete this fill-in-the-bubble, hour-long reading and writing test. (Since then I've learned of Susan Ohanian's opt-out letters. I'll know better next time! In case you don't, go to www.susanohanian.org.)

Scored by a computer in a faraway land, this test was designed to determine my success as a teacher of reading and writing and my students' success at "literacy learning." The score would be sent out to parents midsummer to report on their child's growth as a reader and writer since the beginning of first grade.

I'll never forget watching Robby complete his "bubble-fun" test those two days. It wasn't that Robby didn't know the answers on the test. It wasn't that Robby couldn't read or write. In fact, he flew through the pages saying, "This is easy!" and bubbling in correct answers on practically every question. The problem was that Robby, like many students you know, was an out-of-the-bubble thinker. Those little circles labeled *A, B, C,* and *None of the Above* had Robby's deep, dark, Dixon Ticonderoga #2 marks on the inside—as well as on the outside and all around the circles. Robby needed to make sure those "score people" knew he was *certain* of the correct answer. It's also important to note that six-year-olds, with less than perfect fine-motor coordination, have a pretty difficult time staying in the lines.

The scores came back mid-July and Robby's mom called to report to me that Robby had scored in the twentieth percentile. What's sad about this story is that the scoring computer in the faraway land knew nothing about Robby. It didn't know that way back in September, in that first, very long week of school, I had to practically tie Robby down to practice reading and writing with me. He was the kid who responded, "I don't know" to basically every question I had. And that in June the same child greeted me at the door of our classroom asking for reading and writing conferences and would tell me about the stories he was writing at home each night or the books he needed for his nonfiction research.

That bubble-scanning computer system missed those days I could hear Robby interacting with a text (out loud!), saying, "I can't wait to see what's gonna happen!" or "I knew it!" and the days the intonation in his voice changed as he read stories with varied punctuation. That scoring computer missed writing every day in our class as Robby took the time to write an entire food alphabet book for his kindergarten friends in our last writing study of the year. The incorrect answers on that test showed nothing of the interactions Robby had with his peers as he got suggestions for what each letter in his alphabet book might represent. Little did that test know, but the letter *X* became *miXed fruit* and *U* became *Ugly food* in the ABC book and he used one of his favorite alphabet read-alouds, *Fed Up* by Rex Barron, as inspiration for this piece of writing.

This twentieth-percentile child was the child who understood the ways writers get ideas, that we write for an audience, and that all the writing and reading we do in our classroom is for our world and for a purpose that matters. He left first grade believing he was a reader and an author.

The sad truth is that this twentieth-percentile test score will never be able to show us the Robby we really knew, but will go down in his permanent record and be carried all through school. That's why it's critical to truly assess your students in ways that matter—in ways that teach you, their teacher, about their needs, their abilities, their strengths, and their struggles.

I aree with Paul Dressel's definition of a grade or score as "an inadequate report of an inaccurate judgement by a biased and variable judge of the extent to which a student has attained an undefined level of mastery of an unkown proportion of an indefinite material" (1983, 12). Celebrate your out-of-the-bubble thinkers and commit to meaningful literacy assessment for all students. Bubbles tell us very little beyond who can color in the lines. Children tell us everything.

ADVOCATE

So how can we provide our students with what's best for them if we're required to meet the four-week benchmarks, grade the children on their work, and "cover" brainstorming and drafting and editing and revising and publishing and assessing and celebrating and documenting all in a matter of two weeks and then have our teaching translated into scores published in the newspaper?

This is my advice to you (and it's the advice I keep preaching to myself when my heart starts to pound and my stress level runs high and those report cards or observations or state tests are looming around the corner).

Know your children and know what's necessary to teach them.

What does your state course of study ask that you teach the students in your grade? What does your school require and how does the curriculum grow and change from grade to grade? Learn what's expected of you and know it deep in your heart and bones. Memorize it if you have to. Sleep with it under your pillow. Know your curriculum, your requirements as a professional, and—most of all—the needs of your students, because, as Shelley Harwayne said to a group of teachers in our staff room one day, "If you know the why, you can invent your own how."

Teach and learn what's required the way that works for you and your students.

I get up at 4:00 A.M. and have coffee and check email. My friend JoAnne sleeps till noon, has her pot of coffee in the early afternoon, and checks email somewhere around midnight. JoAnne and I both wake up, have coffee, and check email each day, but we both decide when and how it's done. I learned lots about teaching and learning and life while at the Manhattan New School, but probably the most important thing I learned is that being you, being unique, being the teacher you are while teaching what's expected and what is appropriate for children is what matters most. I quickly realized that I couldn't be Sharon Taberski or JoAnne Hindley or Sharon Hill or Karen Ruzzo or Layne Hudes—those MNS teachers I so strongly admired. But I could be Ann Marie Corgill. We all taught poetry and nonfiction and revising and editing and publishing and celebrating, but we did it with our special touches and our special talents. If your whole grade level is trying to do page forty-two in the workbook on Monday and teach the third expository writing lesson by Friday and have all 142 students hanging their work outside in the halls by next Monday, if you're not already, you're going to be one exhausted, frustrated, and burned-out teacher. That kind of pressure and lockstep teaching can suffocate us all and slowly drain the life out of our work and squelch our love for the profession.

Read and talk and think and process your learning with colleagues and with kids, and teach the curriculum in your way with your students.

Study genres and techniques and strategies in writing, give every student the opportunity to showcase his or her published work (okay, I'm not so sure about doing page forty-two in the workbook), but do all this in a responsible, timely, and developmentally appropriate way. Your way. And if you have to, write an editorial to the local newspaper explaining the rest of the story after test scores are published.

Talk about how to use teaching time and curriculum guides and standards wisely—and how to trim the shrubs.

I remember my third graders in Alabama who named their revising work "trimming the shrubs." That meant that they took out all the unnecessary parts, the parts that didn't add to the meaning or strengthen the craft or lift the quality of their writing. I'm advocating that grade-level and curriculum meetings and faculty retreats and districtwide conference days be devoted not only to developing the curriculum and "beefing it up," but also to trimming the shrubs—taking out all the unnecessary material that doesn't add up or make sense to kids (or to teachers). Teachers will be able to work a lot smarter (notice I didn't say harder) if they are working toward goals that are appropriate for the children they teach. Teachers will believe that their learning and teaching matter if their knowledge and expertise about children is valued. They will not get this support from the administrator who wants everyone on the same page on Monday, or the standardized test score cheerleaders who care more about numbers than children, or the politicians who have never entered a classroom.

Believe that less is more.

Albert Einstein once said, "Any intelligent fool can make things bigger, more complex. It takes a touch of genius—and a lot of courage—to move in the opposite direction." Once you've taken out the deadwood, believe that what's left is important enough to dig deeply into for long periods of time. Give children opportunities to read, explore, practice, talk, and share the writing work they do every day—for significant amounts of time. The deeper you delve into the content and the specifics of the curriculum, the deeper your students' knowledge base will be. When you cover less, you uncover more. Students will then be able to draw from the knowledge they've gained from multiple experiences with books, with writing, and with content-area curriculum over time.

As I've recounted the stories of my students and what impacted them (and me) as students of writing, I realize that although each student and the writing projects they pursued required different tools, different teaching, different texts, different kinds of talk, and different amounts of time, they all needed a teacher who

- Analyzed her instruction and how the child responded to that instruction
- Applauded student work and growth no matter the child's stage of development
- Assisted in all parts of the student's learning process
- Assessed student growth and the success of her own teaching and didn't rely on scores to give her the "real" story
- Advocated for students so that the workshop time each day was brimming with meaningful and productive writing work.

As we move through the pages of this book, you'll see the Six As incorporated throughout chapters. None of these teaching characteristics stands alone. Rather, they all work together to support, strengthen, and "grow" young writers.

In Chapter 2 I will explain the writing goals for the year. Chapter 3 focuses on how I create a learning environment and supply that classroom with writing tools and materials for young writers to grow, and Chapter 4 details the structure of a writing study. In Chapters 5–8, you'll find units of study I've pursued with primary students in grades one, two, and three—from curriculum plans to specific texts and teaching moments to assessment and celebration. Chapter 9 is designed to give you ideas for publication and ways for students to go about producing gorgeous, finished pieces of writing and illustrating.

My plea to you as you begin (or continue) your writing instruction with young children is this: Be that groundbreaking, goal-reaching, mandate-questioning, child-advocating teacher for your students. Be the teacher who creates and teaches and learns in a classroom full of students where differences are treasured, time is honored, and true learning can take place. I walk into my classroom every morning believing this for my students. Let's begin by being the writing teachers our students deserve.

Chapter 2
Writers Will Live Up to What You Expect of Them

I work toward the goal of being a teacher who lives the Six As—a teacher who analyzes, asks, applauds, assists, assesses, and advocates for her young writers. If I strive to exhibit these behaviors myself, I can then support my children in reaching several important goals. Shelley Harwayne always said to the teachers at MNS, "Before you begin, you have to decide what you value." What is it that I hope for or value so much for my students? Before I open the door of the classroom, before we begin the first writing focus lesson, before the first child puts the first word on a piece of paper, I want to know in my mind and heart what I value and expect of the students in my class. I want my students to reach the following goals:

- To love writing
- To see the world with wide-open eyes
- To engage in all parts of the writing process
- To use writing as a tool for communication
- To read and then write a variety of genres
- To see the power of their writing beyond the classroom

To Love Writing

You could search for days poring over state standards or reviewing standardized test objectives or talking to the No Child Left Behinders, but I doubt you would find or hear the objective or the goal "Children will love writing." And since that's one of the sad truths our profession faces today, I'm going to put it in print for you.

Because it *is* important. I would venture to say that, above all else, children should love what they do in school so much that they don't want to do that work only inside the four walls of their classroom. You may be thinking, "Yeah, so what? We all want our students to love school and love what they do in school. But how is that love directly related to their writing growth?"

Have you ever thought about the things you love to do? If you love cooking (unlike me who uses her cookbooks to hold the take-out menus), you want to spend time cooking simply because you enjoy it. It's exciting for you to find new recipes and create new dishes. It's even fun to go to the cooking store and buy new cooking gadgets that will make your meal preparation easier, more interesting, and more enjoyable. You plan dinners and parties for family and friends to share your passion, fill their stomachs, and nourish their souls. The more you take the time to cook, the better cook you become. I know because I lived in a home where my mom's passion for cooking filled my family's stomachs and nourished our souls. She learned from my grandmother and embraced her passion for cooking. The more Mom and Granny cooked, the better they became.

After I moved to New York and came home to visit, I always knew that Granny would have my most favorite blueberry dream cake, with vanilla cream icing and blueberries, waiting along with a big hug and kiss when I opened the door. These special women were great cooks because they cooked often and cooked because they loved it.

My thirty-two-year-old sister has always been a die-hard Bon Jovi fan. I suffered through the music blaring from her room and in the car on the way to school each morning. Life-sized posters covered her bedroom walls; "I ♥ J.B.J." showed up on every notebook or blank writing space. If you had some strange need to know Jon Bon Jovi's favorite color, last girlfriend, or next stop on the current tour, my sister could tell you. She knew every word, every lyric, every new album. Her husband has now so graciously downloaded all the albums on her iPod, and she even recently traveled from her home in Alaska all the way to New Jersey—not to see her sister in nearby NYC, but to sing along in Giants Stadium with the band. All her life she has bought albums, gone to concerts, collected memorabilia, watched videos, sung and sung and sung, and passed that passion on to her family. That love has never died, and when her five-year-old son can sing every word to "You Give Love a Bad Name," you know it.

Whether it's making a blueberry dream cake or belting out a Bon Jovi single, the more you do it, the easier it will become—the better it will taste, the better it will sound. Just as the more writing your students do, the better writers they will become. I know this because for fourteen years I sat alongside children whose strings of letters eventually became well-crafted poetry. I've seen the absence of periods and question marks and exclamation points in numerous drafts, but months later seen these ending marks affect the tone, pace, and mood of a story. I've heard countless children tell me, "I don't know what to write" or, "It hurts my hand" or, "I don't like writing" and then in that same year heard these same children say, "I have so many ideas, it's hard to decide what to do next." Or, "Writing is my favorite. I love it."

To support that writing growth and love of writing, I have to make sure that the writing work we do in class becomes something my students want to do. Like playing a video game or running on the playground, writing may not initially be something that all children are naturally invested in or interested in pursuing. But it's my job to make it that way. Writers deserve to make their own decisions about topic, materials, workspace, and the kind of writing they pursue. When students understand that they are key decision makers in their writing work, it is much more likely that they will grow to love the subject. It's my job to provide experiences that will nurture and encourage students' interest in and love of writing.

To See the World with Wide-Open Eyes

As I think about my students this year, I think about their interests and what's important in their world. Haley loves butterflies and Cam Jansen mysteries. Robby is totally into Webkinz and, with clipboard and pencil in hand, charts all classmates who have a Webkinz screen name so he can send new emails. Mark regularly performs magic tricks for the class and wants to become a magician with a side job as a secret agent. Grace just read *Lilly's Purple Plastic Purse* by Kevin Henkes and, like Lilly, she now has her own pair of movie-star sunglasses to block the rays on the playground. Children's passions and affinities and ways of seeing the world should be honored—by supporting Haley when she wants to write a nonfiction piece about the life cycle of a butterfly; by cheering when Robby uses his Webkinz knowledge to teach classmates how to email each other; by celebrating when Mark writes his first how-to piece on being a secret agent; by being thankful for Bank Street Bookstore suggestions when Grace wants to know what new books Kevin Henkes has written. One way to make sure this occurs is to always give children choice in their writing topics.

In her book *Writing Through Childhood*, Shelley Harwayne writes, "We want children to notice, pay attention, marvel, and be fascinated with the world around them, both in school and outside of school. We also want them to appreciate that what captures their hearts, tickles their senses, and fills their minds, belongs in their writing" (2001, 43). It's important that my students see their lives and their world as a resource for their writing. If children are given choice, they will begin to see the world with wide-open eyes. Their lives will become the palette for their writing.

This choice doesn't mean free-for-all writing with no structures in place and haphazard teaching that doesn't add up. I'm not advocating that. I'm advocating smart teaching that supports students in their smart choices. As we move through the chapters, you'll see how I've balanced choice with structured, purposeful units of study.

To Engage in All Parts of the Writing Process

When I think of state writing tests, I think of how *little* the evaluators and scorers learn about students as writers. It's because these tests require little to no process work. These tests value first and final drafts with correct spelling; immaculate handwriting; proper grammar and mechanics; and, oh yeah, meaningful content (all in forty minutes or less). This isn't brain surgery, folks, where you're taught to get it right the first time. Can you think of a single published author who submitted a first and final draft, with no revisions, no time to think and talk and plan in less than several months? Then why do we expect that of young children? Children deserve to have time to engage in long, focused studies and in the work of *real* writers—writers who struggle with ideas, write numerous rough drafts, misspell and correct words, add and delete and craft their words into stories, poetry, and nonfiction. Learning to write takes time, and the process of writing takes time.

In *Teaching with the Brain in Mind*, Eric Jensen states that "much of what we learn cannot be processed consciously; it happens too fast. We need time to process it. In order to create new meaning, we need internal time. Meaning is always generated from within, not externally. After each new learning experience, we need time for the learning to imprint" (1998, 46). This is why it's important that teachers take children through every part of the writing process and give them time for their learning to imprint.

We live in a fast-paced, fast-food, fast-decision-making, high-tech, sleep-deprived world. Things happen in the blink of an eye, and sometimes we're too busy blinking to see anything. Life passes far too quickly as we rush rush rush to get ahead, step up, reach the top, complete the first and final draft. I want my students to learn that getting ahead, stepping up, reaching the top, means taking the time to slow down, notice, pay attention, and appreciate the process on the way up.

To Use Writing as a Tool for Communication

It's important for children to understand that writers create pieces for *real* audiences and that the purpose of writing is to communicate with your reader. So much of the writing that happens in classrooms today is well-crafted and beautifully illustrated and written for a real audience, but it never goes anywhere. I remember a time in my second-grade class in Alabama when the children and I were beginning writing workshop one day. As the children were getting their materials and beginning their writing work, I was taking a look at the pile of finished work and published pieces that the children had recently written. Just looking at it, it looked like one big mess of papers, and so, thinking "out of sight out of mind," I quickly shoved the class's published pieces in a cabinet to deal with later.

The next day in writing, Conor put the final touches on his piece and proudly wrote "The End" on the last page. He then went straight to that cabinet where the other pieces were, opened the door, shoved his piece in with the others, slammed the door, and went right back to work.

That was the day one child changed my thinking about the purposes for writing and about teaching children that their writing really matters in the world around us. From that day on, anything we did as a class or as individuals was written for someone and was written for a purpose. A poem for Mom's birthday. A reminder note to pick me up from baseball practice. An invitation to my publishing party at school. A persuasive letter about why I don't need to be grounded for a week. A story about my trip to the lake with my grandpa. This is the work of real writers with real audiences. These writers are writing to communicate a message to their readers.

I've also been in classrooms where children are asked to write to people or things that will never be able to read, respond, or communicate with the young writer. Unfortunately, students will never get a pen-pal letter back from the Lion, the Witch, or the Wardrobe. Mother Nature won't write to tell them about the seasons. George Washington has nothing more to say about cutting down cherry trees or wooden teeth. And although Frog and Toad have some cool adventures, reptiles and amphibians in fiction just don't have a lot to say.

Students won't ever see the need to write letters to maintain relationships if they're writing letters to characters in books that won't ever write back. Students will never appreciate a writer's craft or words if they're writing new endings to the Newbery Award–winning novel. Students will never see the need to create an image in the mind of the reader with their poetry if that writing will be shoved in the back cabinet in the classroom never to be read again. What am I trying to communicate? My real readers, I want you to know that all writing in the classrooms of today should be for real audiences and for reasons that matter—for reasons that will add up in the student's writing life in and outside the classroom.

To Read and Then Write a Variety of Genres

It's important that children see the clear connection between the reading and the writing work we do. All reading we do in the class can inform our writing in some way or another. The authors who line the shelves of our classrooms have gone through many of the same processes I want my students to go through when writing clear, comprehensible texts. So, during the year, as we study and learn how to comprehend the texts we read, we also think about how that reading work would strengthen the writing work we do.

Why is it so important that children see the connections in the work they do with reading and writing? While reading *Best Practices in Literacy Instruction* (Gambrell, Morrow, and Pressley 2007), I was reminded that being consistently exposed to different types of literature increases a student's motivation to write the kinds of books they read. First reading and then writing a variety of genres

- ⌀ allows children opportunities to begin to think like the authors they read and have models for specific crafting or illustrating techniques;

- ⌀ helps children focus on structure, layout, and pictures in a text, as well as on content and meaning conveyed by the author;

- ⌀ provides multiple experiences and opportunities for connections to the students' background knowledge and to other subject areas. The more connections students can make through multiple genres, the more they will have to write about. All writing should be based on what children already know, and reading multiple genres is the best way to build that prior knowledge base.

To See the Power of Their Writing Beyond the Classroom

Even if we're writing every day, and writing to publish and share pieces with classmates, parents, and administrators (all within the school building), students are missing one critical understanding about writing: the power that their writing can have beyond the classroom and the school.

Students need opportunities for their writing to go forward and go public—to reach audiences *outside* the classroom and the school—so that they can then begin to see how their words truly affect the feelings, beliefs, and choices of other people in the community, state, and nation. This out-in-the-world writing doesn't have to be writing on a grand scale, but can be anything that gives students a vision for what their words can become. A simple thank-you note to a guest speaker, a pen-pal letter to friends across the country, an invitation to a birthday party are small but important ways to make sure students recognize the power of their words beyond their writing workshop folder at school. Not only are young children far more capable than you could ever imagine, but you'll find that their most passionate and powerful writing comes when they know it will go beyond the unit of study publishing party at school. In Chapter 9, you'll find some of the ways I've worked to give students opportunities to share their voices and their views in writing—beyond the classroom, through the front doors of the school, and out into the world.

Reaching Our Goals: Taking the Tortoise Perspective

According to Webster's dictionary, a goal is defined as "The finish line of a race." Day 180. The end of May or June (depending on your school year and your part of the country) is most certainly the elementary school finish line. The journey will be complete and your class of writers will cross that line. Our students will most certainly reach the goals we set for them back in those warm summer months of preplanning. I am convinced that they will succeed as writers, and we will succeed as teachers of writing, if we will only take "the tortoise perspective."

Remember Aesop's fable "The Tortoise and the Hare"? Slow and steady won the race. It's not because of speed or competition with other students or classes that students will succeed as writers. It's because we keep our eyes on the goals we set, give children opportunities to pursue those goals, and slowly and steadily move toward the finish line. When you pursue writing goals with your students, slow and steady *always* wins the race.

Chapter 3
Designing the Learning Landscape
Providing Space and Materials for Young Writers to Grow

For me, one of the joys of being a teacher is that I get to start over every year. Every June I tearfully say goodbye to a group of students and celebrate their growth as learners. Then I begin to anticipate the upcoming September new year, but not until *after* the beach trip, finishing the stack of unread fiction by the nightstand, and going at least a month without hearing, "Miss Corgill… Miss Corgill… Miss Corgill!" Somewhere in those hot summer months between the June end and the September beginning, I start to think about how to refine my teaching and structure and supply the classroom for the next group of students.

I wouldn't consider myself a big TV fan, but I *am* addicted to the Bravo and HGTV design shows. I also have a special spot in my heart for Ty Pennington and the *Extreme Makeover: Home Edition* design team. In all these shows, the teams start with a blank landscape, an overgrown yard, a dilapidated house—and a vision of what's to come. These teams never work just to design and fill a room, landscape and manicure a yard, or build and furnish a house. They do this work with the people in mind—the ones who will inhabit each space. As the designers begin to plan, build, paint, or garden, I imagine them to first have questions like these: Who are these people that will live in this house or work in this space, and what are they like? What are their interests, their needs, and their passions? How can we make life better and happier and more productive for these people in their new home? I don't have a degree in architecture or interior design, and I'm certainly no Ty Pennington, but I am a teacher who has the opportunity and pleasure every year of creating the learning landscape for a group of children where the living and learning and writing inside those four walls will be wonderful.

With my goals in place and at the forefront of my mind, I can now focus on the classroom environment and physical tools students will need to support not only their writing work, but also their work in all subject areas.

As a writer myself, I get my best work done in an environment that's open, organized, and comfortable. Sometimes I spread my work, papers, and supplies out over the table or on the floor beside me, so that I can see my process and what's already been accomplished. I need easy access to the printer for making multiple drafts to pore over. I need pencils for marking up the text, sticky notes for flagging parts that sound awful, and fresh stacks of bright white printer paper. I need a lamp when the sun outside my window won't suffice, and I need my tiny desk clock to remind me that I need work *and* play time in my life.

I have learned over the years that I can indirectly educate my students by means of classroom environment. The minute a student, a parent, a colleague, an administrator, or a visitor walks into our classroom, my beliefs about what children deserve should speak loudly. As I plan for the children that will inhabit the space, I think about the following classroom components:

Seating arrangements

Library

Storage space

Bulletin boards and wall space

Teacher area and pathways for room navigation

Room colors, lighting, and decorative touches

Writing materials and supplies

Seating Arrangements

Students deserve

- Seating arrangements that facilitate conversations about writing and support the work of writers

- Opportunities to sit alongside the teacher and listen in as the teacher confers with a student about his or her writing

- Comfortable areas to gather when it's time to read a draft, share a published piece, or study the craft of a beloved author

- An environment that values community and the exchange of ideas rather than isolation and self-promotion

- A room that isn't dominated by filing cabinets, large teacher desks, and improperly sized chairs and furniture

I've chosen to fill my classroom with tables and rugs instead of desks. Some tables are round, while others are rectangular. Some are lower to the ground with rugs for seating surrounding them and others include chairs with straight backs. Some are in a quiet nook in the room while others are set up in the middle of the classroom. These tables, chairs, and rugs facilitate the kind of talk, the kind of writing discourse I will teach and encourage. They give the child who likes to work on or near the floor the opportunity to do so. The arrangement also supports the child who needs a straight chair and flat workspace, a quiet area by the books, or the middle-of-the-room energy. It gently sends a message that thinking and learning and working differently together are valued over the mentality that one size fits all or "it's all about me." Our classroom should be *all about us,* and the simple choice of tables and rugs over individual desks is the first step in that direction. But don't panic if you don't have tables and want them. It's very cool how lots of desks pushed together can quickly create that table space that you're looking for. Don't be afraid to make your furniture work for you and your students (or to ask your principal to buy you tables next year and ditch the desks).

Library

Students Deserve

- A rich and varied library with multiple authors, multiple copies, and multiple genres
- A library that's organized with the child's interests, the curriculum, and the teaching in mind
- A library that has the feel of a bookstore, showcasing featured books and authors periodically throughout the year
- A library that meets the reading and writing abilities and needs of all students

Lots of my friends who aren't in education don't quite understand the need to spend hours on the floor of the children's section in Barnes & Noble, Borders, or Bank Street Bookstore. I know. I'll admit it's a sickness, and I do often wonder if I'll ever need the twelve-step program for children's book lovers. Fortunately, it's a very rewarding and productive sickness to have. Because I care deeply about the literature children are exposed to in their years of schooling and because I believe that great books have an incomprehensible impact on students' lives as writers, readers, and people, I stock my classroom year after year with these treasures. But just having the books isn't enough. Doing important work with them is what counts. Reading aloud, rereading favorites, finding new authors to study, investigating the writing lives of the authors—and then writing our *own* texts like the ones we've read. That's what these books are for. They're for the children and me to read, enjoy, and study how these texts are written and created. Since I'm a children's book addict, in the upcoming chapters, I will share some of my most recent (and not so recent) favorites and how we use these in our writing workshop. If you happen to spend your money wisely and aren't magnetically led to the children's section every time you pass a bookstore, there are plenty of other ways to stock your classroom library. Book-club orders, your neighborhood or school library, parent donations, attic visits to find your own children's lost treasures, school funds or grants, class book parties instead of birthday parties, holiday gift wish lists, school book fairs, yard sales—the list goes on and on.

Classroom Storage Space

Students Deserve

- Storage of supplies that are well organized and clearly labeled
- Storage that is strategically separated to avoid congestion and add balance to the room

Storage that eliminates clutter and matches the workspace

Storage that anticipates accumulation, provides space for growth, and eliminates overflow

I've chosen to create separate storage spaces strategically placed across the room rather than have each child keep all his or her materials and supplies in one space. I've found that this type of organization allows me to keep closer tabs on the work in these folders, notebooks, and trays. If I need the class writing folders to study one night, I don't have to go searching in every child's stack of materials to find them, and I don't have to ask children to take time out of our day to locate the materials I need. It also makes for smooth and timely transitions from one subject or activity to the next. I never hear, "I can't find my reading folder!" Or, "Where's my writing folder?" Or, "What happened to my math paper?" because these supplies and materials are always in the same location. The children are responsible for passing out folders and returning them to their proper places, but because each storage space is clearly labeled, that's never a problem. The writing folders are located near the writing supplies. The math folders sit on two sides of the math supply shelf. The reading folders have their home at either end of the independent reading baskets. Reading workshop book bags are housed in baskets in every nook and corner of the room. This way of storing prevents clutter and congestion in one area of the room. There are no extra papers, stacks of unnecessary materials, or random materials from home that sometimes collect in student desks or cubbies. Because these bins and trays can be moved around, I place each one apart from the other so that when it's time to use the materials, there's no crazy traffic jam in one area. I also anticipate the growth of these folders and notebooks as the year progresses, so the bins for storage are big enough to allow for that growth.

Bulletin Boards and Wall Space

Students Deserve

Bulletin boards that have a solid, consistent base color to avoid distraction

Bulletin boards and walls that call attention to the child's work, writing, and art rather than the border, multiple colors, or design behind the work

Bulletin boards and walls that are free of teacher-made or store-bought posters, characters, or quotes

Bulletin boards and walls that are filled only with the work of the children and the teaching that happens in the class

I've always loved drawing and painting and would spend hour upon hour the first few years of my teaching creating things to hang on the walls of my classroom. I had a gorgeous Rainbow Fish, all of Eric Carle's tissue-paper collage characters, and even a giant clown that held the classroom birthday chart. I was never a big fan of the stuff from school supply stores. It took me several years to realize that the classroom could be dripping with *my* artwork and *my* writing and *my* store-bought stuff and not one child would care. No student ever told me how nice my work was or how great I painted in the lines. No first or second or third grader ever commented on my growth as a classroom decorator from beginning of year to the end. It took me a few years to realize that children become invested in their classroom only when it is filled with *their* learning and *their* work. And, boy, did that make things a lot easier for me! From then on, all I needed to do was cover the boards with paper and eagerly wait for the children's work to go up. At first it may seem kind of freaky to start the school year with nothing on the boards or walls, but that vision of what the room can become because of the children always put me at ease and it left space in my teaching life to do more important work—like plan the writing curriculum.

I choose one color now for all boards to create continuity across the room. It's usually black fadeless paper, because I've found that children's work stands out so incredibly on black. I've also figured out a simple way to make a crunched paper border with skinny strips of that same fadeless paper. Each board's border is a different color to match the room's color scheme. I stay away from store-bought border because, basically, I think it's ugly and overpriced. I'd rather spend the money on paper that won't fade and will last the entire year or on a brand-new picture book.

Teacher Area and Pathways for Room Navigation

Students Deserve

- A low-profile teacher area that doesn't take over the classroom space
- A teacher area that isn't always off limits to students during work time
- A teacher area that avoids sending messages of importance
- Clear pathways to and from designated areas in the room
- A room that is free of extra furniture and equipment that isn't used and has no purpose
- Ways to move about the room without a claustrophobic feel or unnecessary congestion

The first year I was at Manhattan New School I had thirty-two students and we lived in close quarters. Class sizes are getting larger and larger and rooms aren't getting any bigger, so it's important for teachers to use their spaces wisely. If a large part of the room is filled with a teacher desk, teacher chair, teacher filing cabinets, teacher corner, then there's little space left for the students to move and work in comfortably. I'm not saying that teachers don't deserve space, because we certainly do. I'm saying that it's important to balance our space with the space our students need. I don't want to send the signal to my students that my needs and my work and my comfort is more important than theirs, and if my area takes up a quarter of the room, then that's exactly the message I'm sending. If I want my students to work together as a community and share the supplies and the workspace, then I should be willing to share my space and materials too.

Room Colors, Lighting, and Decorative Touches

Students Deserve

- A room that feels like a home rather than a hospital, institutional facility, or prison
- A room that is well lit, safe, and comfortable
- A room that honors the work and the learning that takes place
- A room that is clean, organized, and functional
- A room that uses complementary colors and patterns to create a simplistic beauty and a sense of calm

In Eric Jensen's book *Environments for Learning*, he speaks of the effects of lighting, color, and organization on mood, behavior, and cognition:

> Exposure to color, especially bright colors, plays an important role in stimulating and strengthening immature neural connections in the brain's occipital lobe or primary visual cortex… Color is also known to play a key role in the maturation and stimulation of brain areas outside the occipital lobe/visual cortex. (2003, 15)

The areas of the brain that Jensen describes are in turn connected to spatial understanding, emotional message encoding, hearing, language, and memory. In designing learning landscapes, we need to recognize that students' feelings, behaviors, and academic achievement are directly related to classroom environment and the supports provided for optimal academic performance. Because of brain research such as this, I am now able to give specific reasons why I insist on bright lighting, visually appealing color schemes, touches that replicate the home environment, and materials to ensure cleanliness and organization. Plus, students always respond positively to a room filled with their original artwork and writing, rather than store-bought, commercial materials. I've yet to find a child who reads or comments on the stuff that costs a pretty penny at the school supply store. I've never heard a child exclaim, "I love the blank tan walls and the hospital-green tiled floor!" Learning suffers in poor environments, so why not make sure that learning soars in your classroom that's well lit, colorful, organized, and child friendly?

Writing Materials and Supplies

Students Deserve

- A variety of quality materials to support the work of real writers and illustrators
- Access to all writing and illustrating materials at all times
- Places to record and date their daily writing
- Sheets or templates to support their writing lessons and understandings
- Places to house conference notes and writing goals
- Places to document their writing process
- Places to showcase and share writing and illustrating

Luckily, there's a Staples down the street from school and an Office Depot that does overnight delivery in my hometown. I wouldn't survive if I couldn't get my hands on those much-needed office/classroom materials. It's the necessary supplies from stores like these that arrive in my classroom and evolve into purposeful writing tools through teaching, reflection, and use. Over the years, that ream of blank writing paper has evolved into "writing support sheets" and the "weekly writing record." A package of same-color, three-pronged folders has become the "writing journey folder." On sticky note chart paper and foam board hangs the prior knowledge of a class of writers alongside the end-of-unit understandings about a particular genre. Blank bound books have become my reading, math, and writing "teaching point notebooks." It's these seemingly simple, everyday supplies that support the writing teaching and learning in our classroom. Let's take a look at the evolution and use of a few key writing tools and supplies in my primary classroom.

Anchor Charts: Sticky Note Chart Paper and Elmer's Foam Board

I've found that sticky note chart paper and Elmer's foam board are great materials for putting our learning out into the room. At the beginning of a writing study, I chart, "What

We Think We Know About…"This gives me a quick preassessment of the class knowledge of a particular genre or writing study. As we notice, name, and learn specific strategies and techniques for writing throughout a study, I will list our learning on these charts to hang in the room. I love this paper because it sticks anywhere (without removing paint!), and I don't need a stapler or push pins every time I want to hang a chart for the students. As for foam board, I use this for more permanent charts that stay up longer in our room. For example, I might use a brightly colored foam board for an editing checklist, a writing committee chart, or a list of words we use often so that students can refer to it throughout the entire year, rather than just through one particular study.

Rough Draft Folder: Twin-Pocket Poly Folder

Each child in the class has a rough draft folder, typically plastic to reduce wear and tear over the course of the year. The rough draft folder has two purposes: (1) to house any collections, notes, lists, or ideas for writing and (2) to house work in progress until it is transferred to the writing journey folders at the end of a publishing cycle. (More about the writing journey folders later in this chapter.)

At the beginning of the year, we study how writers get ideas and the types of writing they do. The children make lists of possible writing topics. They bring in collections of things that tell a story—whether it be a photograph of the family, a postcard from a friend, a special artifact like a bird's feather or a leaf that means something to the child—things that may inspire them to write about anything from family to the bird they watched in Central Park.

The right pocket of the folder houses the rough draft work. If you looked in any child's folder, you might find a piece of writing the child is working on for publication or it could be several pieces that the child began but hasn't yet completed. These pieces are in progress; the child could be at a variety of places in the writing cycle but the pieces have not yet been published. I ask that the children throw nothing away and save every piece of work unless we have a conference and decide a paper doesn't show their writing growth or support their work toward publication. Every piece they produce in some way shows the journey toward their goal. The steps in the journey are just as important as the destination. These folders will house all the writing and illustrating the children do throughout the study. Each day as they work on part of their piece, I will ask that they date each page so that I can see the progression of the work over the course of the weeks.

The children use this writing folder every day. It's a tool that stays with them the entire year and helps keep them organized on a day-to-day basis.

The Weekly Writing Record, Writing Support Sheets, and Paper Choices: Reams and Reams of Blank White Copy Paper

The weekly writing record is one way the children and I keep track of the work they're doing over the course of each week. We use weekly records in reading and math, and the writing record is much like these two. Each day the children record the title or topic of the piece they're working on and color in the genre circle designating which type of genre they're writing (yellow for poetry, blue for nonfiction, and red for fiction—an idea that came from Sharon Taberski's reading records in her book *On Solid Ground*). This record gives me insight into their writing patterns. Are they sticking with the same topic over several days or do they move from topic to topic each day? Are they focusing on the genre we're studying? (See Figure 3.1 for an example of a completed writing record along with my explanations of what I've learned from it. A blank writing record form is provided in Appendix A.)

A writing support sheet is exactly what its name describes—a sheet that supports the writing work we're doing in a particular focus lesson, guided writing group, or unit

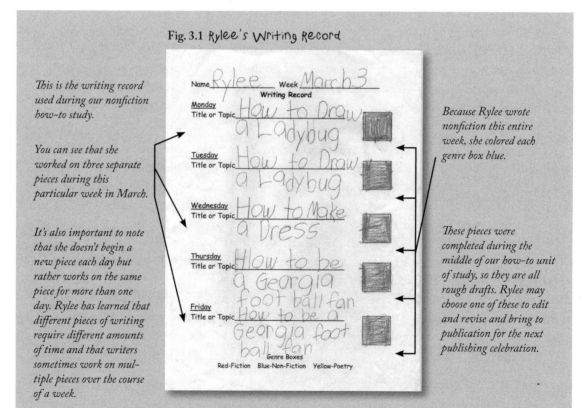

Fig. 3.1 Rylee's Writing Record

This is the writing record used during our nonfiction how-to study.

You can see that she worked on three separate pieces during this particular week in March.

It's also important to note that she doesn't begin a new piece each day but rather works on the same piece for more than one day. Rylee has learned that different pieces of writing require different amounts of time and that writers sometimes work on multiple pieces over the course of a week.

Because Rylee wrote nonfiction this entire week, she colored each genre box blue.

These pieces were completed during the middle of our how-to unit of study, so they are all rough drafts. Rylee may choose one of these to edit and revise and bring to publication for the next publishing celebration.

Adapted from Sharon Taberski's book *On Solid Ground* (2000).

of study. It is designed so that all students have a concrete record of a specific lesson or a visual from my teaching to refer to during their writing work and is a great way to document my teaching and lesson planning throughout the year. I don't use support sheets with every focus lesson I teach, but from time to time I like children to have a written documentation of a lesson or ongoing discussion; this is when I create a support sheet for students to keep in their rough draft folder for use throughout the study. (See Figure 3.2 for an example.)

Fig. 3.2 Josh's Writing Support Sheet

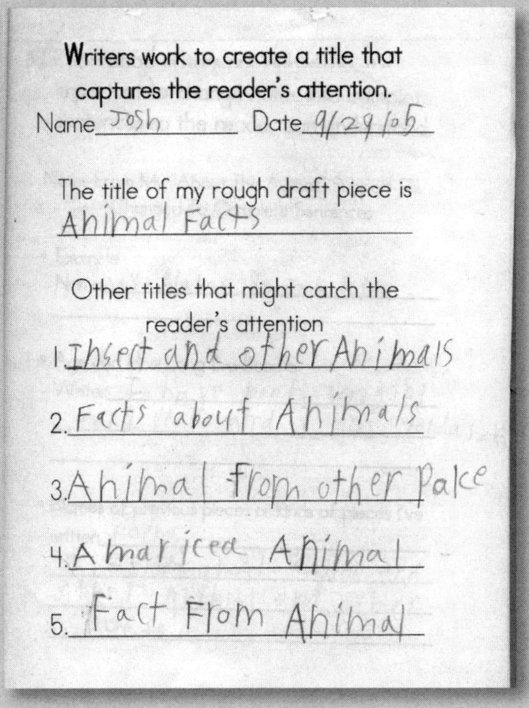
Writers work to create a title that captures the reader's attention.

Name Josh Date 9/29/05

The title of my rough draft piece is Animal Facts

Other titles that might catch the reader's attention

1. Insect and other Animals
2. Facts about Animals
3. Animal from other Pakce
4. Amariced Animal
5. Fact From Animal

I create paper choices in each study that scaffold students in producing both text and illustrations in a clear and organized way, and in a way that matches the genre and the purpose of the piece the child is writing. (See paper choices in appendixes B, C, D, and E.)

Books for Publication and Teaching Point Notebooks: Bare Books

I discovered this source for blank books (www.barebooks.com) while at the Manhattan New School. I saw the students of my colleagues producing these fabulous books, and I learned from them that this was a great way to give published pieces the look of a real book (and, of course, the kids love this publishing option). These hardcover, white books come in different sizes and shapes, with lines or without; are reasonably priced; and are great when you need to bind lots of pages of student work, because the binding is already done for you!

I also use the smallest size Bare Books to house notes and teaching points from individual writing conferences during a specific writing cycle or from guided writing groups. It's a great assessment/teaching tool to share with parents at conference time to show how I specifically taught their child and how that individual conference supported the child's writing work during the study. It's also a great way to keep children accountable for the talk and work that happens during conferences and guided writing groups. Each child keeps his or her teaching point notebook with the rough draft folders so that during writing time, it's easily accessible, and the child can refer to the teaching point when necessary. Students also use this notebook in writing share time to teach the class about their conference, writing goals, and specific teaching point.

Writing Journey Folders: Two-Pocket Folder with Prong Fasteners

At the end of every two- to three-month writing cycle, our class celebrates the published pieces the children have completed. Parents, friends, other teachers, administrators, and visitors are invited in to read the pieces and comment on the children's work. For years I secretly wished that the people at those celebrations could see *every* part of the work that went in to creating each "perfect" published piece. What they always saw were the beautifully watercolored, well-crafted, correctly spelled, neatly handwritten published pieces of writing.

To truly understand the writing journey that each child took, I wanted these people to be sitting next to me the day Jacob needed a conference because he was finished with his rough draft, Caitlin realized she illustrated the wrong picture on the wrong page, Natan was ready to begin his self-reflection, and Grant was still sitting at the table staring at a blank piece of paper. The day we created our first mentor text set. The day I was thinking four-letter words after the focus lesson. The day we "cut and pasted and revised and revised and revised" the drafts. The week before the celebration when there was this writerly hum in the room, not a minute was wasted, and the final pieces were in sight. The day those glue-sticky, marker-covered seven-year-olds were finally able to say, "I'm ready to celebrate my published piece." I wanted these people to see what happened on all these days that enabled the children to grow and strengthen their writing habits, writing pieces, and writing lives.

It's obviously not possible for everyone to actually be in the classroom when all these things happen. But even knowing that didn't make me want to share what happened on those days any less. I needed to let people in on the stories and the secrets of our writing journeys.

There are five parts to the writing journey folder:

- The child's self-reflection
- Rough drafts (editing and revision work)
- Letter to families about the study
- Comments sheet
- Photograph or copy of the final piece

The Child's Self-Reflection

At the end of each writing study, I ask the children to reflect on their work over the past few months on a writing reflection support sheet. This reflection is one of my main tools for assessment of their writing growth. As I read their answers, I learn about their knowledge and understanding of the following:

- The characteristics of the genre we studied
- The purpose of their piece

- Audience
- Specific crafting techniques
- Reasons for revisions
- The use of mentor texts
- Specific focus lessons or conferences that supported them the most
- Parts of their work that make them proud and parts they would like to work on in the next writing cycle

Figure 3.3 shows an example of a completed writing reflection support sheet.

Rough Drafts (Editing and Revision Work)

At the end of each unit of study, the children and I go through their rough draft folders and take out all work that pertains to that unit. For example, if we've been studying poetry, all the rough drafts of poems come out of the folder to be transferred to the writing journey folder. We do this so that parents, fellow students, and administrators can see the rough draft work the children completed in order to get to their final published piece. At the beginning of the year, this section of the writing journey folder is pretty bare. To be honest, I'm lucky if I get anything into this section early in the year since most primary children think that the first draft is *the* draft… *the* piece… *the End*. The rough draft section of the writing journey folder, as with all sections, looks different—becoming more sophisticated—as the child moves through the grades. A first grader's rough draft work looks quite different from a fourth grader's. As the year progresses (and as children move from one grade to the next), they become more adept at rereading their work and really understanding that they are writing for a reader and that their writing has to make sense. Over time, children begin to see that the road to publication isn't a short one, but one that requires lots of writing—and also lots of reading, rereading, sharing, questioning, editing, and revising… The life cycle of a writer is a long one.

Letter to Families About the Study

Since moms, dads, or caregivers can't be in on the day-to-day teaching and learning about writing, I believe it's important to highlight important goals, lessons, and outcomes

Fig. 3.3 A Completed Self-Reflection

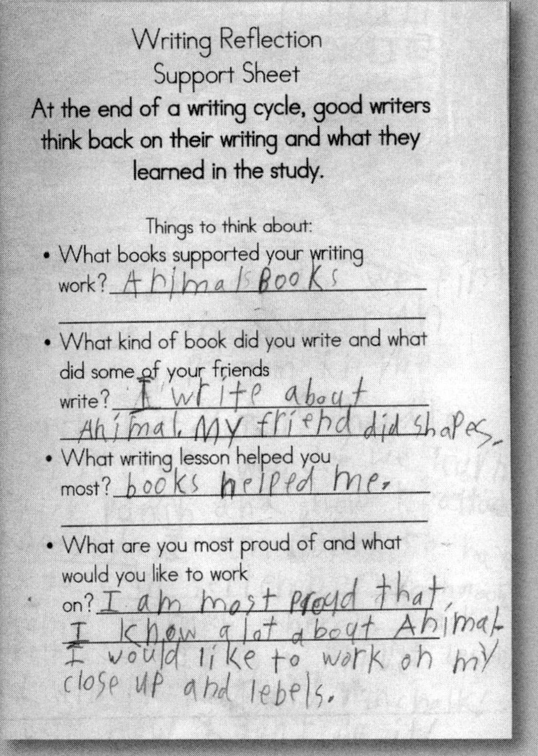

Writing Reflection
Support Sheet
At the end of a writing cycle, good writers think back on their writing and what they learned in the study.

Things to think about:
- What books supported your writing work? Animals Books
- What kind of book did you write and what did some of your friends write? I write about Animal. My friend did shapes.
- What writing lesson helped you most? books helped me.
- What are you most proud of and what would you like to work on? I am most proud that I know a lot about Animal. I would like to work on my close up and lebels.

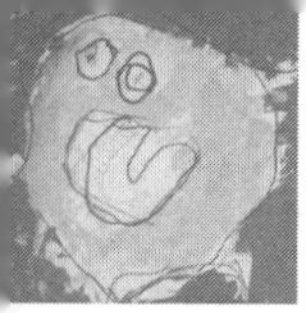

Fig. 3.4 *Letter to Families*

Letter to Families About Our Writing Study

Dear Families,

One of my highest priorities is honoring the work that the children do in this classroom. One of the ways I strive to honor that work is to give children opportunities to learn and grow through systematic, focused, and structured units of study and then to celebrate the work that they have done. This is our first writing-study celebration of the year, and it is my hope that this celebration gives you a better understanding of our writing process and study.

It is extremely tempting to look at what the children aren't doing at this point in the year. You may see lots of spelling and mechanical errors, pages with lots of illustrations but very little writing, and some pages that are a bit out of order. I see these "mistakes" as starting points for growth over the course of this year. I ask that instead of looking at what isn't there, please focus on the learning that has taken place. Their growth as writers will unfold right before your eyes as the months go on and as we continue to share our work with you.

Your children have learned lots in this study, and I am both pleased and proud of the work they have done. The following are some of the things to look for as you're reading their writing and to ask them about:

- Kinds of books/genres that writers write
- Writing topics and what writers do to choose a topic
- How writers help their readers understand and enjoy a piece of writing
- What it means to reflect on your writing
- What other children are writing
- Writing conferences and goals
- How their classmates help
- The Word Wall
- Dedication pages
- Purposes for writing
- Books as models for their own writing
- The way that writing workshop works in this classroom
- The writing journey folder
- How they feel about their work and ways they want to improve during the next writing study

As always, thanks so much for your support and encouragement of the work that we are doing. It is a pleasure to teach and learn with your children.

Happy Rainy Writing Celebration Day!

Love,

Ann Marie

from the units of study we pursue. In these letters I work to include explanations of what adults should look for in their child's writing so that they can see evidence of the teaching that took place in a writing study. In addition to study highlights, I also try to include tips and ways for families to keep the recently completed writing study alive at home. For me, this letter is just another way to communicate our learning to the class community of families and keep the learning that happens at school and at home consistent and reinforced. (See Figure 3.4 for an example of a letter to families.)

Comments Sheet

All young writers deserve to hear comments from their readers, and one of the ways I've been able to document these compliments, comments, and observations is through the use of a comments sheet at each publishing celebration. During a writing celebration, visitors, parents, and students typically move around the room reading the writing of the students in our class. Readers read a piece and then comment on the writing using the comments sheet. This sheet is housed in the writing journey folder and becomes written evidence of the thoughts, ideas, and compliments of real readers. It gives my students one more opportunity to see how their writing has purpose and affects a variety of audiences and readers. From time to time, we take the comments sheets out of the writing journey folders and post them alongside published pieces that hang in the classroom or in the hallways for all to see—and for other readers to add comments to over the time the pieces are showcased in the school environment. (Figure 3.5 shows a comments sheet for a piece of Chloe's writing. You'll find a blank comments sheet in Appendix A.)

Photograph or Copy of the Final Piece

Since many times the child's published piece is either too large or too thick to fit inside the writing journey folder—and more importantly, is too important to hide inside one of the folder pockets—I take a digital photo of the cover of the final piece. The color photo is then glued to the front of the writing journey folder as a reminder of what the final, published piece looks like. This picture becomes a miniature reminder and representation of all the hard work inside the writing journey folder as the real published piece is showcased and shared with audiences across the school, community, or nation.

Table Supplies and Writing Supply Area

Yes, many of the supplies I've just shared with you have evolved into unique teacher/student writing tools for our classroom, but many of the most readily used and available supplies don't become something quite so unique or special. They just do the work they were meant to do, and they are just as important for students to have access to on a daily basis. Permanent markers are meant to outline gorgeous final-draft illustrations. Staples are meant for just that—stapling books and papers together. Pencils are hard at work in the classroom each day writing and revising and editing and drawing and breaking and being sharpened and used again and again.

I vividly remember one writing workshop back in Alabama. Ralph Fletcher was visiting that week and helping me with the writing workshop that day. Rebecca came over to me and said, "Miss Corgill, I need the white-out to fix something in my writing," and I quickly ran over to the cabinet to get the white-out for her. Another student came to me that same class period and asked, "Miss Corgill, do you have a staple remover? I need to take some pages apart in my book," and I quickly ran over to the cabinet to get the staple remover. Ralph was watching all of this, and he finally said to me, "Ann Marie, don't you think that students should have access to all the materials that writers need all the time?" He was right. If my students needed materials, why shouldn't they have access to them? Why was I keeping all these materials and supplies in the cabinet, away from the students? Now that all the supplies are out in the open, clearly labeled, and accessible to all students, the class's writing seems to have more possibility. With the supplies they need, students have more ways to "grow" that writing—and correct it and revise it and illustrate it and publish it—and I'm not running back and forth to the cabinet to get the students

Fig. 3.5 A Sample Comments Sheet

Comments From My Readers	
Reader	Comments
Clara	Chloe, I loved your book because I really learned a lot about you! Also, I love your illustrations!
mom	I LOVED your book. It is very interesting to read about what you like and don't like. You made such beautiful drawings. Keep up the good work.
STEVEN JAY WARREN, PROUD FATHER OF CHLOE MARIE WARREN, A GREAT WRITER/ARTIST	CAUSE, I LOVED YOUR BOOK, ESPECIALLY THE COVER, GREAT JOB. YOU ARE FANTASTIC!!!!
Jinny (Josh's Mom)	You picked very interesting theme and put it very nicely. I love it!

what they need. As far as writing tools and materials go, I give my students a wide variety of choices. In our writing materials area of the room, you will find the following:

- Crayons
- Markers
- Oil pastels, Cray-Pas
- Permanent markers for outlining (both black and colored)
- Watercolors
- Highlighters
- Staplers/staples/staple removers
- Hole punch (two and three holes)/paper reinforcers
- Transparent tape
- Glue sticks
- Scissors
- Sticky notes
- White-out
- Book rings
- Paper clips
- A variety of paper choices (template paper, blank copy paper, and colored paper)

We all know our jobs extend beyond the "teacher" label. I'm sure we've all held the position of nurse, referee, caretaker, therapist, nutritionist, coach, and a host of others at one time or another. Knowing what it takes to get the learning landscape prepared so that a writing community can be established and student growth can occur, I'd like to add architect, interior designer, and environmental protection agent to the list of teacher expertise. The classroom environment and materials chosen to support the work in that room are critical to successful teaching, learning, and writing. The elements of classroom setup and design in this chapter directly relate to the kind of success that will be achieved when building a writing community and the kind of success your students will achieve in their writing work across the school year.

In those hot summer months, when you've come to "prepare the soil for growth," to set up your writing classroom, keep these questions at the forefront of your mind:

- Are furniture and materials developmentally appropriate and strategically placed?
- Is there ease of movement and are there direct lines of vision through the space, from one area of the classroom to the other?

- Are the materials and writing supplies purposeful and convenient to the students and teacher?

- Have you allowed for flexibility in regard to student needs, interests, and abilities in space and materials?

- Is the classroom ready to showcase student writing, projects, and artwork, rather than filled with store-bought, teacher-made materials?

- Is the classroom one of beauty, cleanliness, order, and simplicity?

Remember, real teaching—the teaching that young writers deserve—happens when we put our goals, our materials, our thoughtfully designed classroom, and our young students together. Let the writing growth begin!

Chapter 4
Planning Instruction for the Writing Journey

This past July I packed up the contents of my studio apartment and classroom and moved back to my southern home of Birmingham, Alabama. I filled the car with the items that couldn't go on the moving truck—along with some key provisions for the journey (snacks and water and lots of Starbucks coffee). I then drove for nineteen long hours because my last three flights to Alabama had taken longer than that and I need more than three pretzels and half a cup of watered-down Diet Coke to make it.

Before I departed, I first checked the atlas to see the big picture of where I was going—what major interstates I'd be traveling and what states I'd drive through. Then, I used MapQuest and plugged in starting and ending addresses so I knew the specifics of how to get there: which turns to make, which streets to cross, and which rest stops were along the way. And when I drove into the driveway at 3150 Parkridge Drive, I was finally home! My journey had been safe and successful, and I could begin my "new" southern life.

Just like my travels, my students and I are on a writing journey together, and I have the job of navigator. I'm responsible for planning the journey, keeping us on course, and supporting my crew as we move along. So before I begin a writing year, a writing journey with young students, it's important for me to answer three big questions:

1.   Where are we going as writers this year?

2.   How are we going to get there?

3.   How will we know if our writing journey was successful?

Where Are We Going as Writers This Year?

As I begin to develop the writing curriculum and think about where I want to take students as writers, I revisit my goals outlined in Chapter 2 and plan what I want students to understand and be able to accomplish during each writing study. Examples of my goals, big ideas (important ideas the students need to understand), and essential skills and concepts are found in the curriculum maps at the beginning of Chapters 5–8. Making decisions about what I want to happen by the end of the study—knowing the destination—helps me then be able to plan day-to-day instruction and what we need to do as writers in order to reach these ending points.

When deciding upon big ideas and essential skills and concepts to teach, it's important to first think about the kind of work that is developmentally appropriate for the group of writers at this point in their elementary school career. Depending on the time of year and the student needs and abilities in the class, I make decisions about which aspects to focus on in each unit. For example, in our first study of the year, I spend large amounts of time teaching and learning with my students about how writers get ideas and how to generate writing from day to day. Very little teaching time is devoted to editing and revision in this first unit. First, because my children are five and six, I don't expect them to edit and revise their writing work at this point in the year. I expect them to choose an idea and tell their story without fear of being "wrong" or needing to change lots of things in the piece. If a child's fear of failure and of being wrong overpowers success in the very beginning, then I can fully expect an unsuccessful writing year ahead. This can't happen. I won't ignore teaching children about editing and revision and craft, but I will teach it when it is most appropriate for the learners I work with every day.

Second, I think about the kind of study we're beginning: Is it a study of the habits and strategies of writers? Is it a genre study? Is it a craft study? Is it a combination of all of the above, of both process and product work? For example, if I want students to learn about ways that writers work and to develop strategies for accomplishing their own writing work, then the bulk of my lessons and our talk about writing needs to focus on ways we can learn about and practice these writing habits and strategies. This study wouldn't look like one where we'd focus on the characteristics of a particular genre—unlike, for example, poetry. In a study on poetry, my planning and my teaching are wrapped in the characteristics of the genre. What does a poet's work look like in relation to other genres? What types of poems do poets publish? What crafting techniques do poets typically use? How can we write poems like the authors we're reading?

In every writing study, I work really hard to stick to a short list of big ideas and essential skills and concepts related directly to the unit so that the study is focused and the work (and teaching) is productive, attainable, and successful. For me, it's important to give my students opportunities to do different kinds of writing work and learn about both process and product. It's also critical that I plan the studies so that students have significant chunks of time to devote to writing and learning about the writing in each unit. In Figure 4.1 you'll find my yearly unit of study plan and the time frame for each study.

The finest workers in stone are not copper or steel tools,
but the gentle touches of air and water working at their leisure
with a liberal allowance of time.

—Henry David Thoreau

Fig. 4.1 The Unit of Study Yearly Calendar

Unit of Study	Time Frame for the Study
• Establishing the Writing Community	• Late August–Mid-September
• Where Do Writers Get Ideas?	• Mid-September–Mid-October
• Poetry	• Mid-October–December
• Nonfiction (a features focus study and a procedural writing study)	• January–April (for the two nonfiction studies)
• Combining Our Writing Knowledge (picture books)	• Late April–June

I design my writing curriculum calendar around four or five big writing studies and provide lots of time to establish the writing community and then dig deep into the genres of poetry, fiction, and nonfiction. Each study lasts from four to eight weeks, and students have multiple opportunities to do the things that writers of these different genres do to publish a piece. You won't see us studying poetry for a week and then jumping to how-to books and then on to alphabet books the next week. Young children need time to explore, write, and develop a deep understanding of what it means to write poetry or expository texts or whatever genre or topic they may be studying. So, that's why I make sure that each of our studies lasts for several weeks. I believe that when you cover fewer writing studies in a year, you actually uncover more about each study. With the philosophy that less is more, students come away with a wider and deeper understanding of writing and what it means to be a writer.

As I'm planning our writing journey, I also revisit favorite professional books on the genre or study topic. If we were beginning the school year and establishing the writing community with the children or teaching them what writing workshop actually looks like and what kinds of texts they could create, I might revisit Ralph Fletcher and JoAnn

Portalupi's *Writing Workshop: The Essential Guide* (2001) or Katie Ray and Lisa Cleaveland's *About the Authors* (2004). *Awakening the Heart* (1998), Georgia Heard's professional book on poetry, is dog-eared and coffee stained, as I've reread it countless times while planning my poetry study. Books by Tony Stead (2001) or Janice V. Kristo and Rosemary Bamford (2004) sit on my bedside table when I'm preparing to teach nonfiction writing. It's the work of countless professional authors that ground me in sound writing pedagogy and give me support as I plan fresh, new ways to teach my class of writers and to think about where we're going in our year's writing studies.

As you plan and decide where to go with your young writers, think about the following:

- What work is developmentally appropriate for your writers?

- What kind of writing studies will you pursue?

- What does the year look like in writing? What's the time frame for the studies you want to pursue?

- What professional supports can you use to help you think deeply about your planning and instruction?

How Are We Going to Get There?

I needed lots of coffee, snacks, and bathroom breaks for the trip home from New York to Birmingham. It was also necessary to stop frequently for gas to keep the car going for the hundreds and hundreds of miles I would travel. Key provisions such as these got me to my destination and made the trip pleasant, possible, and successful.

Effective writing instruction also requires key provisions. In the unit of study curriculum maps found in the beginning of each of the next four chapters, I've outlined what I believe are key provisions—the necessities for success in teaching and learning about writing and taking students through the process from rough draft to publication. These provisions are the same for all studies and are critical to the work that happens in the writing classroom every day. Writing time is essential every day, no matter what study you're pursuing. Notice that I didn't say a few times a week or once a week. *Daily* writing is necessary for students to develop stamina, keep their momentum going, make connections to the previous day's or week's work, alter writing plans from one workshop to the next, and see how each new writing day builds on the previous one.

Students also need tools for writing and texts that provide models of the kind of writing they are studying. In Chapter 3, I spoke of the tools that support our work as writers, and I believe it's tools such as these that give students possibilities for their work and the pieces they'd like to publish—paper choices, media for illustrating, texts to provide models, places to house ongoing work, and ways to document the specific teaching and learning that's taking place.

It's not enough to have daily writing time and tools available to the class. For students to grow to their fullest potential as writers, they deserve a predictable workshop structure that gives them opportunities to use the writing materials at their fingertips and to think, write, talk, and share the pieces that they're writing each day.

The Structure of a Writing Study

Writing time in my classroom grows as the children grow, but the teaching in that workshop begins on day one. In a typical first-grade class, I might start the year with a twenty- to thirty-minute workshop period and work up to one hour or more by the end of the year. In each writing study you'll find these key components:

1. Reading for Writing and Focus Lessons
2. Conferences and Independent Writing
3. Writing Share

Reading for Writing and Focus Lessons

Each writing journey begins with lots of reading. Reading and talking about what we notice the writer doing. In *On Writing: A Memoir of the Craft*, Stephen King says, "If you don't have the time to read, you don't have the time or tools to write" (2000, 147). It's important for me to give children time to read and talk about books that are examples of the kinds of writing they will be doing over the next two months. During this daily "reading-for-writing" time, they aren't expected to write the genre, but simply read it and talk about what they notice.

Approximately two to three weeks before a new writing study begins, I collect books for the children to read and talk about each day that relate to our upcoming study. For example, the children in my class might be reading nonfiction procedural texts while finishing up a writing study on poetry. This reading-for-writing time has occurred at different places during the day over my years in the classroom, but it is always separate from our actual writing workshop time. During the writing workshop, I want students writing, illustrating, talking, conferring, and sharing their writing. Reading about the genres they write is critical, but I don't want that reading time to engulf the writing work we should be doing every day. That's why I devote a separate time just for reading the kinds of books that are examples of the genre in which we are trying to write. It's important to note that because we begin writing on day one, it isn't possible for students to read before they write in our first study. So, at the beginning of the year, I use our read-aloud time during the day to introduce children to these books and the area of the room where they will find the reading-for-writing shelf. They will learn that this will be the place books about our upcoming writing studies will be housed and that they will be reading for writing from this shelf throughout the year. (See Figure 4.2.)

Fig. 4.2 The Reading-for-Writing Shelf

In previous years, the children began the day reading as writers, and we used part of our morning meeting time to chart "noticings" about the genre we were planning to write. This year, however, students read during the last part of my word-study block while I work with a small group, and then we gather to share. During this time I ask children to look for the following:

- Ways the words are written on the page
- How the writer uses illustrations or photographs to support his or her writing
- Interesting language
- Choice of text or font sizes
- Purpose of the writing
- Topics the author writes about
- Intended audiences

In the upcoming unit of study chapters (Chapters 5–8), I discuss charts the children and I have developed during this reading-for-writing time and you will see examples of some of them. These charts then guide our work as we begin to write the genre in upcoming weeks and become the crux of our focus lessons every day before writing.

As I mentioned earlier, I typically devote two to three weeks of reading before the writing study begins, but it's important to mention that we continue that reading every day through the study. As the children begin to write and craft their texts, these books are used more and more often as supports for the children during their work. They notice more about craft, style, voice, layout, and purpose, and they talk more about what they're doing in their own writing and how it's like the work of an author they've read. They begin to place their own writing alongside the work of beloved published authors and recognize that they are authors themselves.

Conferences and Independent Writing

During the independent part of the workshop, I have one-on-one conferences with students. I find conferences the hardest yet most beneficial part of my teaching. I have to confess that I am a bit of a perfectionist and very much a preplanner. (Okay. Honestly, I am over the top in my perfectionist tendencies and struggle daily with learning to just chill out. I don't do spontaneity and have this need to know what's coming.) All that is shot to hell when I have a conference with a kid. For me, writing conferences remind me of those Miss America on-stage interview questions. You never know what question they'll ask, but you know it's going to be big, and Miss Alabama better have a good answer because her beauty won't make up for sounding dumb.

In writing conferences I never know what the child is going to say or what question he or she will ask. But I know it's going to be important to the writing work, and I better come up with a smart way to teach that writer. And yes, it's ultimately my teaching—not my good looks—that will help this child.

If you expect every conference to go amazingly well, to say the exact thing the child needs, to balance your talk with the talk of the child, to know immediately what this child needs and what to do to move his or her writing forward, then you've got issues with perfectionism too. Let's both get over this, because the perfect conference isn't going to happen every time. But don't let that stop you. Instead of thinking "perfection, polished, planned," think "assess, applaud, assist." In my conferences, the best way to get better at teaching the children is to practice teaching them. Just like I ask them to write every day and practice what they've learned, I have to practice conferring. First, I work to get a sense of what children need by asking questions or having them share their writing with me. Every day I practice making a quick assessment of what the writer I'm meeting with is doing or needing support with. (Videotaping yourself is a great way to grow stronger in your conferring abilities.)

Conferences are purposeful when you really listen to the writer. It's important to let the child's needs guide you and not be guided by what you think you should say just because it's "got to be covered" in writing or because that's what it says to do on day two of the unit of study.

I've also learned that no matter what, it's important to confirm and applaud what the young writer is doing well. It may be extremely difficult to find that one good thing, but find it no matter what. Words like, "It's so smart to remember to put the date on your paper. That helps show us how much you've grown when we look back at this piece," or, "Your color choices for this illustration are so interesting. What made you choose purple, green, and pink for your house?" or, "You are really helping me understand your writing better when you put spaces between your words!" give young writers confidence and show that you respect and validate their thinking and writing. You're much more likely to see them go off and try to improve their writing when they think they can do it.

It's also critical to make sure the conference teaching point or plan of action is practical and succinct—and that the child can actually use what you taught when they go off to work independently. We all know that when you confer with a primary writer and read their work, there are numerous teaching points that jump out at you, and it's tempting to deal with them all at once. Don't give in to that temptation. Pick one thing to teach, and teach it the very best you can. Some days I may feel that my conferring skills are a bit rough around the edges, but I do know that it's in these conferences that students have opportunities to share their writing with me and ask questions. I try to send them off with one plan of action for their work that's purposeful and practical. While I may vary some parts of my writing conferences, the following parts are always included:

- Ask what the child wants to talk about in his or her writing or how you can help.
- Listen first and assess where the writer is in his or her process and what the writer needs.
- Applaud and affirm some part of the child's writing or illustrating work.
- Decide on *one* teaching point.
- Assist the writer through teaching-point talk, support sheets, or demonstration.
- Ask the child to restate the teaching point or plan of action in his or her own words after the conference is over.
- Ask if the child is willing to teach the class and summarize the conference in writing share.

I begin each conference with the questions, "What do you want to talk about in your writing today?" or "How can I help you?" This lets the children know that I expect them to have something to talk about and that one of the ways growing writers can improve their craft is to talk about ideas, strengths, and struggles. Next, I listen to what the child says, and this is the part that can be a bit tricky or unnerving for me at times—this is when I have to very quickly decide how to best help the writer in front of me and be very careful not to jump ahead before I listen to all the child has to say.

I learned long ago, that teaching the *writer* and not the writing is the only way to get children to produce better writing. If I'm busy correcting spelling and giving multiple suggestions for improving the piece and reworking parts for the child, then I'm not teaching the child. I'm just making the writing better or different. Then, the writing becomes mine and not the child's. It *is* my job to give children strategies and supports that they can use not just in the piece at hand, but also in other pieces or work they might be pursuing in the future. My teaching points are general enough so that children may use the teaching long after the conference is over.

I go about this teaching using our teaching point notebooks first discussed in Chapter 3. Each child keeps this small, blank notebook in his or her writing folder, and every time I have a conference or guided writing group with that child, I record notes to myself about the conference and the child's teaching point inside. I have never been great with keeping up with assessment folders or three-ring binders containing children's assessments and conference notes. The years I tried this kind of record-keeping were the years that I had a lot of notebooks and folders filled with blank pages and very little record of the individual teaching that happened.

Now, after lots of trial and error, I've found what works for me—and, more importantly, what works for my students. Students keep their teaching point notebooks in their writing folders, and I am no longer in charge of keeping up with them. The notebook is not just a place where my notes are found, but it also houses each teaching point the child uses to support his or her work after our conference as well as my "teacher research" from each conference. This notebook has changed my teaching and has supported my communication with parents. It's a great way to document individual learning and is perfect to share with parents at conference and report-card time. At the end of the year, the child takes this notebook (or notebooks) home as a yearly record of the learning and teaching he or she did as a writer. I have recently expanded this idea to my reading and math workshops, and it has both simplified my record-keeping and enhanced my teaching tenfold.

If you're wondering what the other children are doing while I'm conferring, they are writing. It's that simple. There are no magical center activities the kids are rotating through to keep them busy as I do individual teaching or small-group work. I'm trying to simplify my teaching and get the most "bang for the writing buck," and I can't do that if I'm spending my weekends making up multiple things for kids to do. And kids certainly aren't growing as writers if they aren't writing. "Do a Cute Activity" is not a descriptor in Bloom's Taxonomy nor is it on my list of essential writing skills and concepts.

I work very hard to make sure that the work we do in the classroom is something that children will do outside our four walls for the rest of their lives. People in our world write letters and poetry and novels and nonfiction and prescriptions and movie scripts and letters to the editor. I can't think of a single profession where adults go to work and rotate through center activities. So that's why I expect children to be writing and doing things that writers do while I am meeting and talking with individual students about their writing.

Writing Share

At the end of our independent writing and conference times students put away materials and join me on the rug to revisit the work that happened that day in the workshop. Typically, the students who had conferences with me lead the share time. I'll say to the child, "Say back to the class what we talked about in our conference." This is the way I know that the child still understands the teaching point and his or her responsibility and plan as a writer. Also during writing share time, the child reads the piece and receives questions or comments from classmates, and then I ask him or her to "teach" the class his/her own plan of action. This reteaching time is a way to draw the entire class into the teaching of that one conference—to give them all new strategies for working and improving their pieces. As the child completes the share, he or she then asks the rest of the class this question: "Can anyone say in their own words what you just learned from me today about writing?" I'll encourage two or three children to say aloud what they learned and how they interpreted the teaching in this child's conference. All this talk helps bring our writing language and habits and strategies out into the room, and that daily talk about writing not only teaches the children with whom I confer, it also supports and teaches the children that I don't get to spend one-on-one time with that day. We've also gone so far as to showcase these plans of action in the room so that there's a visual representation of the talk for all to see. (Figure 4.3 shows how these plans of action were displayed.)

Fig. 4.3 Plans of Action Showcased in the Room

My first graders and I created the following list of questions and statements that you might hear as the children talk during our writing share time:

In my conference today, Miss Corgill and I talked about . . .

I'm working on _____ in my writing today.

In my conference today, Miss Corgill suggested . . .

Today in writing I learned . . .

How can my conference with Miss Corgill help you with your writing work?

What did you learn about me as a writer today?

What are your questions?

Does anyone have any comments about my writing or suggestions for my writing work?

I liked the way you . . .

I'm confused. Can you please explain why you did _____ in your writing?

I have a suggestion/question/compliment.

My teaching point from the conference is . . .

Who's your audience and what's the purpose of your piece?

Could you please speak more loudly?

May I speak?

Excuse me, but I think I hear other people talking while I'm trying to share.

Who would like to start the share?

Thank you for your suggestions and comments. I may try to use some of those in my writing.

Teaching the big ideas, the essential skills and concepts, and the crafting techniques happens in all parts of a writing study—in reading and noticing characteristics of the genre, in focus lessons, in independent writing and conferring, and in share time. These parts can't stand alone, but rather build on one another and make for whole, purposeful, predictable teaching.

How Will We Know if Our Journey Was Successful?

At the end of a study, I assess the success of my teaching by studying three parts of a child's writing process:

1.   The writer's published piece

2. The rough draft work

3. The writing reflection

At the end of a unit of study, each child will proudly share one piece of writing that he or she has taken from a simple idea to publication. This piece is the first symbol of the writer's success. It signifies weeks of work learning about a genre, attempting writing strategies and crafting techniques, engaging in editing work and revisions, and making decisions about how to publish for an audience and a purpose. It's in each piece that I can see the successes of our writing journeys.

It's not just in the final, published pieces that I am able to analyze and assess student success in a writing study. I also look at each young writer's beginning work in the study, daily drafts, and work over the course of the weeks of the study. How did this child come to the topic choice or the decision to publish this piece? How do these drafts differ from the final piece? Can I see growth in content, craft, editing, and revision from these drafts to the final piece? If I can answer these questions and point to specific ways the writer grew through the pieces, I celebrate this success in their work and in my teaching.

Finally, I am able to assess the success of each child's writing journey by reading and studying the writing reflections. Through these, I learn about children's ability to reflect on their new learning and new knowledge. It's important to always applaud and celebrate growth—whether it's a tiny step or a giant one. A crayon design in the beginning of the year is worth celebrating. A name and date on rough draft work each day is worth celebrating. When *ct* in a rough draft becomes *cat* in the published piece, that's worth celebrating. A picture with a few words that grows into several pages of connected words and pictures and a final published piece—that is cause for applause and celebration. Any step forward deserves applause and the acknowledgment of success (not just for the child, but for you, the teacher.) All writing growth, no matter how small or how grand, signals that both teaching and learning are taking place, and that, my friend, deserves a standing ovation!

In upcoming unit of study chapters, you'll see examples of growth from rough draft to final piece to the writing reflection, and you'll be able to see our successes and our mishaps and not-so-successful moments—all of which are important in teaching and learning and "growing" young writers. Teaching is a lot like traveling, because when traveling, we all know where we want to go, but sometimes there are bumps in the road, flight delays, detours, or those many necessary bathroom and snack breaks. Despite all the obstacles, and with a ton of patience and persistence, we eventually get where we're going and are successful in our journey.

As you embark on your writing journey with your students, remember to trust yourself and remember that you are the person who knows your students best. You are decision-maker, curriculum developer, teacher, and coach. What I've written in these unit of study chapters worked for my students in my classroom, but no unit was ever exactly the same with each new group of students. From class to class, from one writer to the next, I changed lessons, added parts, found new writing models, had different discussions, but I always taught the *writers* in my care. Let's remember that we are not teaching a curriculum. We are teaching children.

I am not afraid to say that there are many scripts and guides and curricula out there today that are little more than nonsense under a glossy cover in a shrink-wrapped $300 box. I've seen them. I've shuddered to think that school districts actually buy and force their teachers to use this stuff to "teach" kids.

But I've also seen and read and used curriculum guides and kits written by experts in our field that are grounded in relevant research and what's best for children. There's no doubt that these materials are produced in the name of supporting the teacher and the children in the classroom. That is the key word: *support*.

We expect our students to think and negotiate and wonder and question and read and write from what they know. If we expect these behaviors from our students, then we should expect the same of ourselves. I say this to you, because I have written the following four chapters in a way that gives you multiple ideas and opportunities to do just that—think, negotiate, wonder, question, and teach from what you know. You will not be given a day-to-day explanation of our writing studies or told what to say. I am not advising you to stand in my shoes and do what I do. These chapters are designed to *support* your *own* thinking and work in the teaching of writing.

It is my hope that they will support you in knowing where to go, in understanding how to get there, and in celebrating your successes as teacher and coach of a class of young writers.

Chapter 5

Establishing the Writing Community
Routines, Tools, and Writing Strategies

Establishing The Writing Community: Unit of Study Curriculum Map

Key Provisions (what students must have)	Big Ideas (what students need to understand)	Essential Skills and Concepts (what students should be able to do)	Possible Text Supports (what students might use to support their work)	Assessment (what students will complete as documentation of growth)
• Topic choice • Daily writing time • Opportunities for writers to read the kinds of books they want to write • Demonstration, practice, teaching, and celebration during workshop period • Opportunities for writers to write a variety of genres • A purpose for writing and an audience • Support from the other authors and teachers in the classroom (students, teachers, books by published authors) • Tools necessary for writers to write and publish the kinds of pieces they envision • Time for writers to think, talk, write, and share every day	• Writers develop routines or regularly followed methods for writing and working each day. • Writers respect their writing environment and take care of tools and materials that will support them in their writing work. • Writers develop habits and strategies to support and enhance their writing.	• Work independently on writing for a sustained amount of time • Develop a topic using pictures, words, or both • Demonstrate knowledge of the basic characteristics of a book (title, author, writing, ending, author's note, etc.) • Share pieces of writing with classmates and teach them new learning • Give and receive comments, suggestions, and questions about writing • Explain the purpose and audience for their writing • Be familiar with the topics of other writers in the class • Write multiple rough drafts and make a choice for publication • Publish one piece for class celebration	• *The Puddle Pail* by Eliza Kleven • *Low Song* by Eve Merriam • *I Am an Artist* by Pat Lowery Collins • *Anna's Table* by Eve Bunting • *A Box of Friends* by Pam Munoz Ryan • *The Way I Feel* by Janan Cain • *That Makes Me Mad!* by Steven Kroll • *What Makes Me Happy?* by Catherine and Laurence Anholt • *Courage* by Bernard Waber • *My Dad* by Anthony Browne • *Wilfred Gordon McDonald Partridge* by Mem Fox • *Imagine* by Bart Vivian • *Imagine* by Alison Lester • *I Want to Be* by Thylias Moss • *What's Up, What's Down* by Lola M. Schaefer	• What We Know About Writers and Writing chart (pre- and poststudy) • Student work samples from beginning, middle, and end of study • Videotapes of writing share and conferences during the study • Rough and final draft work • Writing journey reflection

I vividly remember one writing share in the beginning of the year—one that solidified my thinking about how to start a year with primary writers. Imagine this: It's the first few weeks of school and we're in one of our first writing share times. Owen, a blond, freckle-faced, toothless wonder, proudly hops into the chair at the front of the room to read his first published piece. Using two sheets of red construction paper he found in the writing materials area with pages haphazardly stapled together, he's ready to share his writing and he knows how to command an audience. "I'm waiting until everyone is ready to listen. This is a good book! It's about how to make a snowflake!" Classmates are seriously attentive and ready to hear his writing when Owen shows them the title ("HaW two mAc A SnO FLAC") and his one-page book (so carefully illustrated in white crayon). "This is a snowstorm that has lots of snowballs and snow on the ground. The end."

As Owen takes questions and comments from his audience, Ella, one of my more precocious writers, quickly states, "Owen, you said your book was about how to make a snowflake, but you didn't teach us how to do it." And Owen's quicker-than-lightning response in his six-year-old Alabama accent was "Well… how am I supposed to do that? I ain't never seen snow before in my life!"

Owen's comment in writing share that day reminded me that you can't expect kids to do things that writers do or act as writers act or write pieces with meaning and purpose if they don't have any knowledge or experience in doing so. In order to have a productive, successful, joyful writing classroom, our first units of study with primary writers need to be ones in which we help our students learn new classroom writing routines, how to use new writing tools, and how to develop successful writing strategies. It's important to teach young students those things that they don't yet know about writers and writing and haven't had experience with, but it's also important to help them recognize that the things they do know so well—their lives and experiences—can be resources and reasons for their writing.

For the first month and a half of school, we learn (1) classroom writing routines and how writers work and act in a writing community, (2) what tools a community of writers uses to support their work, and (3) what strategies the young writers in that community can act on when creating a piece of writing.

Creating a Routine

Let's begin by going inside our primary classroom in the first week of school. But before we do, let me say this: Beginning anything is never easy. Beginnings are messy, unpredictable, and scary. Think of the painter beginning the portrait. Think of the baker beginning the cake. Think of the runner beginning the marathon. A lot of paint and a blank canvas. A lot of eggs and cups of flour. A lot of muscle aches and many miles ahead. But what drives these people is that they can envision the end product. The lifelike portrait. The melt-in-your-mouth birthday cake. The record-breaking twenty-six miles. It is the same for us, the teachers of writing. Beginning our year with primary students is messy, unpredictable, and scary. But what drives us is what's ahead after a year of quality writing instruction. What's ahead are students who work and act as writers; produce well-crafted, gorgeous pieces of writing; and choose to write purposefully for the rest of their lives.

But let's go back to day one, week one, month one and remember things are really messy and scary before they become pretty and accomplished. In order to create a writing routine in your classroom with your students, the most important thing you can do as a writing teacher is begin on day one—give the kids paper and pencils and crayons and markers and say, "We're going to have writing time every day in our class, and it's going to be really great." Or you might say, "Just write! Our writing time this year is going to be lots of fun!" No doubt there will be lots of talking and lots of questioning and lots of chatter in the room—"I don't know what to write" or "I'm finished. What do I do now?" Lots of "Where are the crayons?" and "Can you sharpen my pencil?" and "How do you make the stapler work?" There will be broken pencil points and crayon marks on the tables and glue-sticky hands and paper covering the floor. And, yes, you may seem a little fried and overwhelmed at the end of it. I know. I feel that pain every August or September (and even into October!), and it's normal. But don't give up. Establish a writing routine on day one and stick to it.

Our classroom writing routine lasts approximately one hour and always includes a focus lesson, independent writing and conferring time, and writing share. The routine is the same every day except for differences in the time allotment of that hour over the course of the year. At the beginning of the year, we tend to need more time for focus lessons and settling in to our writing at the beginning of the workshop period as well as time for cleanup and share at the end of the workshop period. The children need longer amounts of time to practice the routines of passing out writing folders, finding appropriate materials for work, and settling in to their actual writing. We also need extra time for cleanup at the end of the period, so that children can make sure that their writing work and all materials are in their proper places and ready for the next writing day. At this point in the year, although settling in to write and cleanup take more time, we need less time for actual writing and conferring until the children build writing stamina and can focus their attention on the writing work. As their stamina increases and they develop strategies for writing and producing pieces, the length of the writing time increases. At the beginning of the year, our independent writing and conferring time lasts around twenty minutes, and by the end of the year, we have built up to at least forty minutes of independent writing and conferring time (see Figure 5.1).

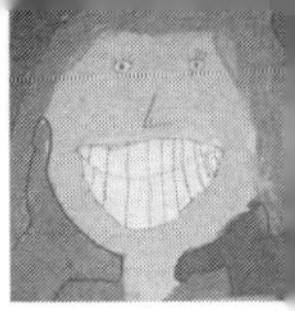

Fig. 5.1 Writing Workshop Routine

Beginning of the Year	
Our Writing Workshop Routine	**Time Frame**
Focus Lesson/Settling In to Work	15 minutes
Independent Writing/Conferring	20–25 minutes
Share/Cleanup	15–20 minutes
Midyear to Late in the Year	
Our Writing Workshop Routine	**Time Frame**
Focus Lesson/Settling In to Work	10 minutes
Independent Writing/Conferring	40 minutes
Share/Cleanup	10 minutes

As you live and work through these days of writing chaos at the beginning of the year, try to take a step back and really listen to the questions being asked and what caused the chaos at the writing materials area or during your conference time with a student. Everything that's happening is an opportunity to teach (and then go home that afternoon and have a glass of wine!).

It's in these early months of writing workshop that I can just hear myself saying (in a very strong and serious voice), "I am *trying* to hear your classmate read his writing, but you're making it very difficult for me to hear!"

I can't count the times I've said, "I'm *shocked* that you don't care enough about your writing work and fellow writers to use a quiet voice." But we are teaching five- and six- and seven- and eight-year-olds who make sense of their world through talking, and the more we let them in on the problem solving, the more respectful and productive they will become. "What can we do about those times when I'm conferring with a classmate and I can't hear him over the room noise?" "What can we do to respect the other writers in this class during workshop time?" "What does a productive writing workshop look and sound like? Do you think we can try that today?"

From Trouble to Teaching Point: What Problems Did We Come Across Today That Can Help Us in Our Work as Writers?

Peter Johnston (2004) says that when we ask students questions like the one above, it implies that it is normal to encounter problems in a classroom. Every teacher and every class does. This, in turn, makes it normal to talk about identifying, confronting, and solving those problems, allowing students to view them as places to learn. It also sets up the possibility of asking, "How can we solve that problem?" Framing the question like this reminds the student of his or her agency, that "I can do something about this."

At the heart of the "I'm going-to-pull-my-hair-out" teaching moments, try to remember that with problems and mistakes come teaching opportunities. Children learn not only about how to change negative behaviors into positive ones, but also about writing and the work of writers at the same time.

When Calvin staples his finger instead of his book

How can this problem help us with the use of the stapler? It's at this point that a series of our writing focus lessons are on stapler use. I teach the children where the stapler and extra staples are housed in the classroom. They learn how to load it when it's empty and what to do when it becomes jammed. They learn how to staple (and not slam) the stapler into their pieces of writing, and keep their fingers out of the way at the same time. They learn how many pieces can actually be stapled together with our less-than-fancy Swingline. They learn where writers typically staple their books. We even have lessons on removing staples with the staple remover, which is also located in the writing materials area.

When Antonio accidentally glues every page in his writing folder together

How can this problem teach us about using glue sticks? Learning how much to roll out of the tube, how to glue corners, how not to go "glue-stick crazy" with ridiculous amounts all over the paper are all lessons that are necessary. Even learning how to make sure your paper doesn't look "hunky and bumpy" with massive amounts of glue chunks underneath is a lesson. Seems crazy, but so necessary to eliminate those glue catastrophes.

When Rylee confiscates all the colored permanent markers or when it looks as if a Fifth-Avenue ticker-tape parade has just marched through the classroom

How can these problems help us learn how to distribute and use only necessary materials and learn cleanup procedures and expectations? Lessons on distributing and returning workshop materials in a timely and effective way are critical to efficiency and productivity in writing workshop. I've learned by trial and serious error to make sure that all writing materials are not in one area of the classroom, but that they are housed in strategic and separate locations so that there's not a mad rush to one area of the room each day when writing begins. Writing folders are in a separate basket near our whole-class rug area so that a few students can pass them out while others are finding spaces to work or gathering materials needed for writing that day. Paper is organized by different types (plain copy paper, colored sheets, construction paper, writing template papers, and so forth) in cubbies or writing trays so that students can see the paper options in each slot and where to return unused paper. Each table in the room has community writing essentials—tools necessary for writing every day, such as pencils, erasers, crayons, and colored pencils. All other materials are housed in separate containers for easy access and organization, and the children learn to gather only the materials they will need right away and return what they are finished with to the proper place. This ensures that we have fewer and fewer comments and questions such as, "Miss Corgill! Jack's keeping all the markers and won't let me have one!" or, "Where are the scissors?" or, "We lost all the paintbrushes!" Learning to share, use, and respect the writing materials in the classroom makes for cooperative young writers who are autonomous, productive, and willing to negotiate. And it allows you to be able to seriously teach and support the writers in your classroom for the rest of the year instead of being a writing referee each day.

When writing workshop becomes a time to make paper crowns and Scotch-tape swords and construction-paper armor and then march to lunch as The Class That Lives in La La Land

How can this problem lead us into a discussion about the work that's happening in writing workshop?

In teaching writing, it's critical for us to be prepared (and to be okay with) the days (and weeks) where there are bumps in the writing road and things don't go as smoothly as we planned—or at all like we planned.

For example, take my first month of this year in first grade. My plan for the journey is to support children in writing and learning strategies for getting ideas and producing pieces that reflect their lives and experiences. This will be my eleventh year to launch a writing workshop (thanks to Ralph Fletcher and JoAnn Portalupi, who got me started in my third year of teaching), and I am confident in my expectations and plans. I have books by authors who share their experiences with their readers. I have brand-new writing folders and lots of paper choices. Sharp pencils and crayons fresh out of the box. I have focus lessons planned and high hopes for this first publishing cycle. I imagine this group of first graders gripping pencils and telling their stories in letter strings, approximated spellings, and lots of pictures—all eagerly getting to their writing work each day.

Not even close. Instead, I learn quickly that I have a group of children far more interested in the stapler and scissors and tape, and in our first week of writing workshop, instead of a class of writing folders filled with work, I have a class of six-year-olds wearing paper crowns and necklaces and superhero belts to lunch and for the rest of the afternoon—and being extremely proud of their "writing" work that day. I borrowed the words of Katie Ray and Lisa Cleaveland and told my students on that first day that writing workshop is a "happy place where we make stuff" (2004, 1). And, needless to say, my first graders interpreted those words *very* differently from what I had hoped or expected.

I quickly realized that my plans for this first unit of study needed to be altered quite drastically. Before we could write about our experiences, we first needed to study what it meant to actually write. Instead of stapling crowns and bracelets together, we needed to learn how to use the stapler to connect pages of a book. We needed to learn that markers and crayons make illustrations to support our words and our stories and that red markers aren't meant for fake blood on our arms and legs. (And this is when *I* learned that we needed a separate art time during the day when children could create and play with the art supplies!)

There are so many goals, objectives, and outcomes thrown at us in the name of leaving no child behind; however, it's important for us as teachers to choose which goals, which lessons, and what kinds of assessments are appropriate for our students. Sometimes we have to take several steps backward in order to move our young writers forward. *You* are the teacher, and you know better than anyone what's appropriate and engaging for the young writers in your class. Remember that.

I would love to watch the politician who mandates that specific benchmarks be met by the end of the first month of school try to tell Calvin to use the red marker for paper and not for fake blood. I'd love to have the "no child left behinders" step in my shoes the day Grace cries because she really *needs* the stapler, the day Owen hides Cooper's writing folder under the carpet so we spend the first part of writing workshop searching for Cooper's materials, the day Chloe accidentally sends her final draft through the paper shredder. Life happens in writing workshop and all day long in the elementary classroom. Trust yourself, meet your kids where they are, and don't simply rely on a script or a packet or a "first-grade curriculum" that someone has given to you. Your children will teach you what they need. Follow their lead.

Teaching Your Growing Writers

Over the years, as I've moved with my students in grades one to four through beginning-of-year writing studies, I've created numerous charts and detailed lists of writing routines, ways to use tools, and writing strategies for young students. No matter the age or the grade of the writers I've taught, my attention isn't directed simply to those routines, tools, and strategies, but, most importantly, to the growing writers in my care. For me, being a writer, being a learner, being a teacher isn't about "arriving" and finally knowing it all. It's about growing stronger and wiser and more confident and independent in the work you pursue. Every person who puts words on a page is in some ways growing toward a new goal—whether it's to meet the deadline for the newspaper one hour earlier than last week, to finish that last chapter of a first novel, to revise the second paragraph of page two for the five-hundredth time, or to simply get out of bed and turn on the computer. Adult writers are still growing writers, and young children need to know this too. I want my children to understand that, just like the authors we read, they are growing by writing every day—whether it's thinking of an idea, adding another sentence to a piece, illustrating to tell a story, or simply choosing paper and finding a pencil to begin work.

With adults and children, the growth is different but the lesson is the same. Growing happens in the doing. If we don't act, we don't grow. I want my students to recognize this. I don't want them to think that they will one day wake up and realize there's nothing more to learn. I want them to wake up and realize that today is another chance to grow. Everything we encounter, every lesson we're taught, every experience we have is another opportunity for us to grow. It's because of this belief that my focus lessons and conference teaching points begin with the words *Growing Writers*. Beginning my teaching this way sends a clear message to my students that this teaching point or focus lesson is just one of many routines, tools, strategies, or lessons that will help them grow in their writing abilities.

Possible First Focus Lessons and Teaching Points for Growing Writers

At the beginning of the year, these first few days are typically filled with statements from the children that begin with "I don't" and "I can't" and "I won't" and questions that begin with "Can I?" "May I?" "Will I?" My response to all these statements and questions is *yes*.

Yes, you will be able to think of something to write.

Yes, you can spell this word.

Yes, you will be able to finish this piece.

Yes, you can write whatever you want.

Yes, you can use all the writing supplies.

Yes, you can talk and draw first.

Yes, you can write on any paper you wish and use as much as you wish.

Why is my answer such a confident yes? Because these are the things I will teach my students in this unit of study. We will learn together how to use tools and materials, we will develop a writing workshop routine, and we will discover and use the strategies of the authors who line the shelves of our classroom, of the authors who come to speak at our school, of authors that sign books at the bookstore, and of the young authors that sit at the tables in this classroom. The way this happens is to simply turn the questions, statements, and needs of my young writers into focus lessons and conference teaching points.

Here are some examples of teaching points I've developed with previous classes that helped us launch and sustain a productive writing time each day for an entire school year.

Examples of focus lesson topics about writing tools and materials that I might talk about with my students at the beginning of the year precede each teaching point.

Writing name and date on papers each day

Growing writers put their name and date on all pieces of writing. (We want to see your writing growth, and dates make that growth clear!)

Hearing the "pop" as students close the tops on the markers and pens to prevent drying out

Growing writers listen for the "pop" when replacing the marker and pen tops. (Dried-out ink means no more markers and pens!)

Returning rough drafts to writing folders when it's time to stop writing for the day

Growing writers place all papers faceup in their rough draft folders. (Loose, mixed-up pages slip, fall, and get lost!)

Using writing tools in careful and respectful ways

Growing writers use a gentle hand when stapling papers together. (Banging hurts the stapler!)

Choosing paper, replacing unused sheets in the trays at the end of the workshop time, and recycling

Growing writers take only the paper they will need and know they can always go back for more. (We are not in the tree-killing business!)

Knowing what to do when you find a lonely writing utensil or material out of place

Growing writers keep papers inside their folders and tools in the proper places when they aren't doing writing work. (This writing behavior stops the "I can't find it!" comments, and we don't want the custodian sweeping up our important work!)

Making choices about where to sit and engage in productive writing work

Growing writers find a place to work where they can do their best writing. (A fooling-around writer is not going to grow as a writer!)

This next group of focus lessons was generated from typical questions that come up each day as we work as writers. You will find the question and then the lesson that resulted from it. These are lessons that also support the development of general classroom procedures and management techniques. What works for writing and is expected in the writing workshop also works for reading, math, social studies, and science.

How often do we write?

Growing writers write every day.

Where do I keep my writing?

Growing writers keep their writing in a place that is personal and safe.

Where do I find writing materials?

Growing writers know what materials they need for work and know where to find those materials. (See the photo of the materials area in the color insert.)

What do I do in writing workshop?

Growing writers can read, think, plan, write, or talk about their writing during workshop time.

Where do I sit when I'm working on my writing?

Growing writers find places that are comfortable, quiet, and supportive to do their writing work. (See the photo in the color insert of areas of the room set aside for writing work.)

What do I do when I'm finished with my book?

When growing writers finish a piece, they start a new one. Writers write lots of rough drafts before publishing.

What happens when writing time is over?

Growing writers know that when writing time is over, they clean up, organize work/papers, and store materials for the next writing time.

Fig. 5.2 How Can I Help? Chart

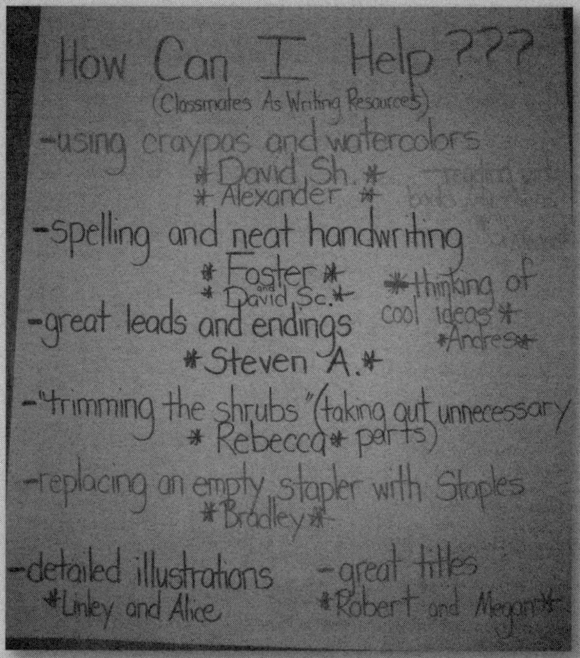

How Can I Help ???
(Classmates As Writing Resources)
-using craypas and watercolors
    David Sh.
    Alexander
-spelling and neat handwriting
    Foster   *thinking of
    David Sc.   cool ideas*
-great leads and endings   *Andres*
    Steven A.
-"trimming the shrubs" (taking out unnecessary
    Rebecca parts)
-replacing an empty stapler with Staples
    Bradley
-detailed illustrations   -great titles
Linley and Alice   *Robert and Megan*

When I teach these lessons, I emphasize that I am not the only teacher in the room. I show children specific ways to get help and support with their writing without relying only on me. It's important that young children learn to use all their resources and find ways to teach and be taught even when I'm not front and center. (See Figure 5.2.)

One of the best ways for children to have writing support is to talk with their peers. During the workshop, children are engaged in their own writing but are encouraged to share and talk about the writing and illustrating they are doing with classmates. They get ideas, give ideas, make comments, reread work together, and learn about each other as writers and as people. So you see that the word *teacher* is much bigger than me. When you are planning instruction, think about the ways to use all your resources because you are only one person and can't do it all alone. Let your children rise to the occasion and take responsibility for the learning *and* the teaching too.

Below you'll find examples of questions children might have about using the resources in the room to support their writing, and the teaching points and focus lessons that resulted from these questions.

How do we share our work?

Growing writers share their work in progress with table partners or in whole-group share time for comments, suggestions, and compliments. (Our ideas sometimes come from the writers around us!)

What do I do when I need Miss Corgill, and she's having a conference with another classmate?

Growing writers know that one-on-one conference time is important and respected, and they find a friend for help when Miss Corgill is having a conference. (Everyone in this class is a learner and teacher, and learning and teaching time cannot be interrupted!)

What is a mentor text?

Growing writers use books they've read to give them ideas for writing.

Who gets to share?

Growing writers develop a sharing routine so everyone has equal time to read and show their writing.

What does the audience do when a fellow writer shares his or her piece?

Growing writers know that during share time we ask questions and make comments and suggestions to the author. (Questions require an answer from the author. Comments and suggestions are statements made to the author of the writing.)

What happens when I have a conference with my teacher?

In a conference, growing writers may ask for help, share thoughts, and develop plans and next steps for writing or illustrating.

Yes, primary students need to learn all these "simple" tasks *first* in order to get to the nitty-gritty work of crafting and developing the ideas, language, and content of a piece. I do confess that sometimes all I can think is, "This kind of stuff is taking so much of my teaching time!" and "I need to get to the meat, the real curriculum!" Yes, I still have these thoughts. With all the pressures of content coverage and meeting the standards, we sometimes forget that it's in the seemingly tiny or insignificant parts of our teaching that we are building the strongest foundations for our students. We all have to let those panic moments wash over us, because what we're really doing here is getting our students ready to engage fully in the context and content of writing as well as meeting and surpassing the writing standards.

Teaching these kinds of lessons first will free you up to have productive one-on-one conferences and guided writing groups without being interrupted with, "How do I staple my book together?" or, "The red marker is dried out and I need it to finish my mom's lips!" You'll have multiple opportunities to help build autonomy and self-directed learners when you suggest that students go ask a friend or look at the How Can I Help? chart and see who's good at using watercolors. These "management-before-meat" focus lessons will allow you to sit in the back of the classroom and watch your group of students lead the writing share time and facilitate questions, comments, and suggestions for the writer. Remember, it's okay (actually it's more than okay; it's brilliant) to have a focus lesson on how to put the crayons away in the table bins. It's so smart to teach children how to place their paper in their rough draft folder. I can't tell you how happy you will be that you spent a few focus lessons teaching children how to date their papers when you're looking back and assessing their writing growth over the year. Because you've taken the time and care to teach these little lessons that have big implications for how the rest of the year will run, you are now able to focus on teaching children how to become stronger writers—writers who use the tools and materials in the room wisely and independently. These early teaching moments are of primary importance to the success of your workshop the rest of the year.

What Are the Students Writing Every Day?

When I think of our writing experiences in the beginning of the year, I am reminded of times when I taught swim lessons to kids in the neighborhood each summer. In order to teach these children, I had to first let them get their feet wet, have the time to get used to the water, and trust that I would be there to help them float when they felt like sinking. That's the way it is with my primary writers in this first unit of study. These kids need time to get their feet wet: to explore what they know through oral storytelling, writing, and illustrating; to try out the materials in the room that a writer might use; to learn classroom writing routines; and to engage in the process of real writers every day for a predictable period of time. If children love what they're doing, they will naturally work harder on the task at hand and grow stronger in their writing abilities (Routman 2005).

I believe that children should write on day one and write every day until day 181. I'm not an advocate of teaching them everything you think they should know and *then* letting them write. This beginning of the year work is the time to hook the children, to give them perfect materials, perfect tools, perfect writing opportunities, and reasons to beg for writing each day.

It's usually not until after several weeks, or even that first month of school, that I begin to feel comfortable that the children have a solid grasp of how to use the materials in the room. By this time, the children typically have pieces in their folders that don't look a lot like books—and often don't even look like writing at all. It's normal (and wonderful) to find pages with only illustrations or lots of letter strings, blank papers with simply a name and a date, and lots of paper stapled together. Because what really matters at this point in the year is that the room is humming with a joyful writing energy and the children are confident that the work they are doing is the work of real authors.

Fig. 5.3 *Cover of Mina's Book on Feelings*

After the first several weeks of school, I begin to see the children negotiate and solve problems on their own. I see them begin to make deliberate choices about paper and materials. I listen in on the talk and the work that's happening at each table, in each corner of the room. At the table by the window, Dylan is writing a piece about his summer vacation to Martha's Vineyard, and an oblong green blob in the middle of his paper stares me in the face. "That's it! That's Martha's Vineyard!" he exclaims. Mina is using Jamie Lee Curtis's book *Today I Feel Silly and Other Moods That Make My Day* to craft her own piece titled "How Do You Feel?" (Figure 5.3) while Brooke is across the room drawing the cover to her "opposites" book, "Down Is Where the Flowers Grow, Up Is Where the Birds Go" (Figure 5.4), inspired by *What's Up, What's Down* (Schaefer), our read-aloud from earlier in the week. Nan is intently focused on her big chapter book about four girls and a lost puppy (Figure 5.5). "I'm already on chapter three!" she announces. Griffin says, "Illustrators draw pictures better with a very sharp pencil!" as he moves from his seat to the pencil sharpener for the fourth time that morning. I can smell the permanent marker ink. I can hear the chatter as a group of my primary writers read their work to each other. I can look across the room and see the wheels turning in these little minds, and for another year, I happily sigh as I think…, "3… 2… 1… *Liftoff!*"

It's then, when the room is up and running with beginning writing work, that I focus my attention, my whole-class instruction, and my individual conference time on teaching children specific strategies for creating, sustaining, and publishing complete, content-filled pieces of writing for the rest of the year.

Fig. 5.4 Cover of Brooke's Book on Opposites

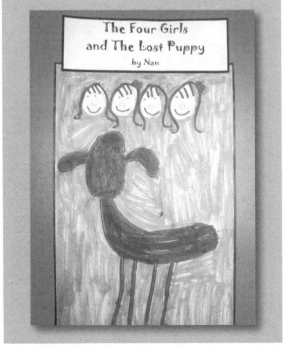

Fig. 5.5 Cover of Nan's Chapter Book

Where Writers Get Ideas: Unit of Study Curriculum Map

Key Provisions (what students must have)	Big Ideas (what students should understand)	Essential Skills and Concepts (what students should be able to do)	Possible Text Supports (what students might use to support their work)	Assessment (what students will complete as documentation of growth)
• Daily writing time • Opportunities for writers to read the kinds of books they want to write • Demonstration, practice, teaching, and celebration during workshop period • Opportunities for writers to write a variety of genres • A purpose for writing and an audience • Support from other authors and teachers in the classroom (students, teachers, and books by published authors) • Tools necessary for the writers to write and publish the kinds of pieces they envision • Time for writers to think, talk, write, and share every day	• Writers use their world and their experiences to discover and collect ideas for writing. • Writers write for different purposes and different audiences. • Writers use their reading and the work of other authors to gather ideas and discover possible formats for their own writing.	• Collect photos, artifacts, and writing to represent their lives and their experiences • Draw, paint, and create a self-portrait collage • Talk about writing and art with classmates in share time • Decide on and develop a new topic using pictures, words, or both. • Explain the purpose of, the audience for, and the root of a writing idea • Be familiar with the topics of other writers in the class • Write rough drafts and make a choice for publication. • Choose a writing format and publish in that format (e.g., ABC; Opposite; Question/Answer; Beginning, Middle, End; Poem) • Publish one piece	• *Hooray for You* by Marianne Richmond • *Whoever You Are* by Mem Fox • *The Puddle Pail* by Eliza Kleven • *Low Song* by Eve Merriam • *Anna's Table* by Eve Bunting • *A Box of Friends* by Pam Munoz Ryan • *The Way I Feel* by Janan Cain • *That Makes Me Mad!* by Steven Kroll • *What Makes Me Happy?* by Catherine and Laurence Anholt • *Courage* by Bernard Waber • *My Dad* by Anthony Browne • *Wilfred Gordon McDonald Partridge* by Mem Fox • *Imagine* by Bart Vivian • *Imagine* by Alison Lester • *I Want to Be* by Thylias Moss	• What We Know About How Writers Get Ideas chart (pre- and poststudy) • Student work samples from beginning, middle, and end of study • Videotapes of writing share and conferences during the study • Rough and final draft work • Writing journey reflection

Beginning-of-Year Strategies: Using Our Resources to Get Writing Ideas

"I don't know what to write!" "I don't have any ideas!" "What can I write about?" "I can't think of anything to write!"

Sound familiar? If you've taught any group of students, it's likely you've heard these statements and questions from the young writers in your care. Our job as writing teachers is, number one, to help our students answer these questions, but most importantly, to help them in a way that doesn't create a class full of writers reliant on the teacher for every idea and suggestion. If we want our children to live in the world as writers, readers, problem solvers, and autonomous human beings, then we have to create a writing environment that teaches children to use the resources around them to support their work and learning. *Webster's* definition of a resource is "a new reserve supply that can be drawn upon when needed." Our work in helping children get writing ideas should be based on the assumption that we're not giving them ideas but making them aware of the writing around them so that they can draw upon these resources when needed—and find writing ideas and possibilities for their own work when the time is right.

Strategy One: Writers Use Their World and Their Experiences as Resources for Their Writing

> *Students need to know what kinds of things writers do,*
> *throughout the process, to get their writing done.*
> *They need to know strategies for getting ideas… for publishing.*
>
> —Katie Wood Ray

Our beginning-of-year writing workshop is filled with lots of time telling the stories of our lives and our experiences. I recognized the vastness of a young child's world and the unique perspective young children have on their world and the moments in their lives when my nephew Jack visited me in New York City this past year. I couldn't wait to spend three days seeing New York through the eyes of a five-year-old. But I was also *not* looking forward to the very close quarters with family in my 500-square-foot studio apartment.

Within minutes of arriving at the apartment, Jack covered every square inch of the studio (which took all of five seconds) and immediately exclaimed, "Wow! Your home is huge!"

Now we all know that Jack wasn't talking about my less-than-spacious living quarters. He was talking about my place among millions in this amazing city. I could just imagine how big the Big Apple seemed to Jack when as an adult, the city seemed many times overwhelming to me. Perched upon my bed, looking out the twenty-ninth-floor window of my apartment into the glowing city skyline, Jack was right. This place was huge! It was a big moment for a little guy.

Just like our young writers, the little people that inhabit the space of our classrooms every day, the moments in the lives of five-, six-, and seven-year-olds are anything but small. They're *big* moments in a world filled with opportunities for remembering past experiences and making new memories each day. Thanks to Jack, I recognized that the moments in a young child's life are anything but small, and it's this beginning-of-year writing work that teaches children that their short histories, the "big moments" in their lives, are important resources for their writing work.

To help them make the direct connection between their lives and the multiple possibilities for writing from their experiences, the children engage in a "self-portrait collage" project during our social studies time, in addition to their daily writing time. Specific information and materials for this project are found in Chapter 9. This project allows each child to teach me and his or her classmates through drawing, painting, collage work, and talking. As my class of first-grade sword, crown, and mask makers so clearly reminded me, young children love to make stuff, and this self-portrait collage project is a way to grab their attention and help them begin the writing year not only as storytellers and artists, but as risk takers—with little fear of not being able to write or publish. This first publication is more a piece of art and a springboard for talk than a piece of actual writing. But that's where primary children need to begin—with lots of support and success with what they have had experience with and *can* do.

Over the first few weeks of school, along with the pieces they're writing in writing workshop, we use the children's self-portraits during writing share, asking for questions, comments, and compliments about his or her self-portrait collage or writing. At the end of each share time, you might hear me say, "Wow, Mark certainly has an interesting life. There's lots there to be written about! I noticed that several of you guys were interested in Mark's picture of himself in the magician's costume. He told us about his magic tricks, so maybe he could write about some of those tricks and teach us how he does them?"

It's this "possibility talk" that begins to give the children ways to look at their collage work, illustrating, and daily writing as the seeds or roots for future writing work. Our share time at the beginning of the year is devoted to bringing writing possibilities and stories to the surface, but don't discount those morning unpacking-the-backpack conversations, chats to and from the lunchroom, and the Monday weekend recounts that can all translate into possibilities for writing from experience. We work to recognize the big moments in the lives of the young writers in our classroom, and I help them see their lives as the number one resource for writing work. See Appendix B for a sheet that supports beginning writers in writing about things they care about and also for the reflection sheet we use for the first published writing students do.

Strategy Two: Writers Think About Audience and Purpose Before Writing

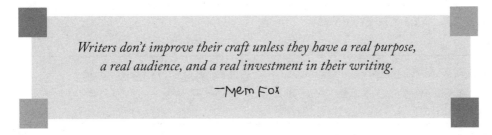

Writers don't improve their craft unless they have a real purpose, a real audience, and a real investment in their writing.

—Mem Fox

My students need to know that when they are writing, their main goal is to communicate a message to an audience. They are always writing for others to understand their message—whether it be to entertain, to inform, to persuade, or to maintain relationships, the ultimate goal for the writer is to communicate with their readers. In our classroom, the reading we do is directly related to the writing, so it's important that my students see how these two aspects of literacy work together. As a reader, we want to understand or comprehend the writer's message, and as a writer we want to write a message for a reader to understand.

The chart in Figure 5.6 was developed with my students over the course of the year. In both writing and reading lessons, we refer to this chart and I might ask questions such as these: "What writing practice did you use today to help your reader comprehend your text?" "How does that work connect with your reading?"

Fig. 5.6 Comprehension Practices of Readers and Writers

Practices Readers Use to Comprehend Texts	Practices Writers Use to Write Comprehensible Texts
Bring background knowledge to the text when reading	Brainstorm, collect, and create writing ideas based on their background knowledge
Come to the book with a purpose—to be entertained, instructed, informed, etc.	Ask the questions, "What's the purpose of my piece?" "Who's the audience?"
Use text organization to better understand fiction, nonfiction, or poetry	Organize the text so that the reader will know if it's fiction, nonfiction, or poetry
Visualize to get a clear picture in their mind of what they're reading	Use clear, detailed language, illustrations, and word placement to help the reader visualize
Use word meanings, word structures, phonics knowledge, and punctuation to comprehend	Edit for spelling, punctuation, capitalization, and word choice
Reread when a part of the text doesn't make sense	Revise when the story, meaning, purpose, language, or organization doesn't make sense
Talk about their reading with others—question, comment, and listen; read fluently	Share (fluently) their writing, asking classmates to listen, question, and comment on the piece of writing

Strategy Three: Writers Use the Work of Other Authors as Resources

The best way to learn to write is to study the work of the men and women who are doing the kind of writing you want to do.

—William Zinsser

In our classroom, writing and learning about what writers do, where they get ideas, and why they write doesn't just happen in that hour-long workshop period each day. Every morning after the children enter the room, unpack, and get ready for the day, their first stop is at the reading-for-writing shelf. In the beginning of the year, the shelf is filled with books that support the following teaching points about where writing ideas come from.

Growing writers are "idea collectors."
The Puddle Pail by Eliza Kleven
A Box of Friends by Pam Munoz Ryan
Anna's Table by Eve Bunting
Treasures of the Heart by Alice Ann Miller

Growing writers sometimes write about their feelings.
The Way I Feel by Janan Cain
That Makes Me Mad! by Steven Kroll
When Sophie Gets Angry—Really, Really Angry by Molly Bang
Today I Feel Silly and Other Moods That Make My Day by Jamie Lee Curtis
What Makes Me Happy? by Catherine and Laurence Anholt
Wemberly Worried by Kevin Henkes
Some Things Are Scary by Florence Parry Heide
Courage by Bernard Waber
Serendipity by Tobi Tobias

Growing writers sometimes write about their families, friends, and pets.
My Dad by Anthony Browne
My Big Sister by Valorie Fisher
A Weekend with Wendell by Kevin Henkes
Loki and Alex by Charles Smith

Growing writers sometimes write about their memories.
Sweet, Sweet Memory by Jacqueline Woodson
Wilfred Gordon McDonald Partridge by Mem Fox

Beekeepers by Linda Oatman High

The Sunsets of Miss Olivia Wiggins by Lester Laminack

Growing writers sometimes write about their dreams and future plans.

Imagine by Bart Vivian

Imagine by Alison Lester

I Want to Be by Thylias Moss

Growing writers sometimes write about the places they live and the world around them.

Whoever You Are by Mem Fox

My New York by Kathy Jakobson

City Kids: Poems by Patricia Hubbell

Who Is the World For? by Tom Pow

The Meet the Authors and Illustrators series is also a great source for letting your young writers in on the secrets of the published authors in the room. Books by Patricia Polacco, Eve Bunting, Cynthia Rylant, Lee Bennett Hopkins, and a long list of other writers give the children information from the writers themselves about the process of writing and where ideas and plans for books come from.

The books on this shelf are chosen for students to read to each other, to read with me in small groups, or for me to read aloud to the class as a whole. We use these books to facilitate talk in our share time each morning, to serve as the foundation for a discussion on writing, or to model what's possible in writing lessons and conferences. At the end of the reading-for-writing time each morning (usually lasts about twenty minutes), we gather as a class for our morning meeting. Part of that morning meeting time is devoted to a discussion about the books the children read, what they discovered or noticed about the writing, the topic, or the structure of the book. I then help the children transfer what they've noticed into possibilities for their writing work later in the day.

For example, I might read aloud *The Puddle Pail* by Eliza Kleven (a book about two dinosaurs that collect the things they love) and use that book to support a writing teaching point for the day—either in our morning writing share, in a focus lesson, or in a conference with a child. The teaching point might go something like this: *Eliza Kleven helps us understand that growing writers sometimes write about their collections.* Or, *Growing writers sometimes collect ideas like Saul and Ernst did in* The Puddle Pail *before using part of that collection for a piece of writing.* Or two children may sit side by side and read *Wilfred Gordon McDonald Partridge* in reading-for-writing time one morning and then share that book at share time. I then use their share to teach, *Growing writers sometimes write about their memories.* Or maybe a simple question from a student in our reading-for-writing share turns into an opportunity for teaching about writing. For example, the question, "What is a mentor text?" might transfer into the teaching point: *Growing writers use books they've read to give them ideas for writing.* The books and the discussion that results from them support our work as both writers and readers, and the students come to trust the authors who line the shelves of our classroom as mentors and friends.

Please know that I'm not advocating that every student use the information we've discovered in our discussion on that particular writing day. It's not reasonable or developmentally appropriate to expect all primary writers to use every teaching moment to enhance their work. But I do believe that it is reasonable and developmentally appropriate to expect that this daily discussion is building a student's background knowledge about writing, the work that writers do, and how published authors communicate with their readers.

At the end of writing each day, we think back to one of the strategies we've learned, and I ask students to either think about or answer aloud the question, "What writing strategy did you use today to support your work or to help your reader comprehend your text?"

Once the students have generated ideas and have topics or genres to pursue, it is then that you can look ahead to new studies of specific genre, craft, editing and revision, and content-area writing.

In Conclusion: Listen to the Voices in the Community of Writers

When beginning a year with young writers, remember the importance of teaching lessons about seemingly simple materials, routines, and strategies. Lessons that don't seem so big in your grand writing plan—like learning when to sharpen the pencils or how to pass out the writing folders or where to put rough draft work—when accompanied with daily writing time will become the foundation of all student writing success and accomplishments over the year. The management work you do first will set the stage for what your young writers are capable of accomplishing throughout the year. Keep your strategy instruction simple at the beginning of the year, and teach your students ways to begin and sustain their writing work for days at a time. These first studies may have that messy, out-of-control feel, and that's normal and necessary if you are to learn about each of your students and their passions and abilities as writers—and, most importantly, to hook them on writing and help them develop a love for the subject.

As I think back to the many years I've launched a writing workshop and supported the formation of a community of writers, the lessons I've learned as a teacher bring me back to one Saturday afternoon walking back from Central Park in New York City. That summer afternoon I decided to take the city bus back to my apartment on East End Avenue. I found myself waiting at the Madison Avenue bus stop with a little lady dressed in Bermuda shorts and a straw hat, with a thick and glorious Southern accent. "Hooooney, da you know whut aaaall theeese pO-lice bahhrrriicades aaah doin heah?" (In case you didn't know, that's south Alabama language for "Honey, do you know what all these police barricades are doing here?") Delighted to hear a voice from home, I quickly engaged in conversation and told the lady I thought they were from the parade that marched down Madison Avenue earlier in the day, and then I asked, "Are you visiting the city?" "Noooo, hooneeyyy. IIIII've liiivvved heah foah yeahs." And I replied, in my own accent, "Me too, and I just can't lose the southern accent." "Wherah areah you froooommm?" asked my fellow southerner. I replied, "Thomasville, Alabama." By this time I knew exactly who I was talking with as I stared in amazement and she replied, "Weeelll, IIII'lll beee. IIIII'm frummm Monroeville" (a town about twenty miles north of my hometown of Thomasville). That day, in one of those New York City moments, I had met, ridden the bus for several blocks with, and chatted with Pulitzer Prize–winning author of *To Kill a Mockingbird*, Nelle Harper Lee.

We didn't talk about *To Kill a Mockingbird* that day, but we did talk about big-city life, our Alabama homes, and the butterbeans she was on a quest to find that day. We both realized that it's not so easy to find butterbeans on a hot summer's day in New York City, and I realized that my "To Kill a Mockingbird Moment" would be one I would remember and connect with for a long time. Harper Lee didn't know it, but that experience with a world-famous author helped me to articulate the power of my own writing instruction with primary students.

I'm taken back to the part of her book where Atticus says to Jem, "Remember it's a sin to kill a mockingbird." Miss Maudie later explains to Scout that "mockingbirds don't do one thing but make music for us to enjoy. They don't eat up people's gardens, don't nest in corncribs, they don't do one thing but sing their hearts out for us" (1999, 103). Many times our students come to our classes with no chance to have their voices or their songs heard. They're left to mimic and produce formulaic, step-by-step writing. It's heartbreaking to see an entire class of five-paragraph essays all beginning with the same topic sentence. To me, this sends the message that no child has the ability to think of his or her own beginning sentence or way to craft an interesting essay. I've watched children with anxious eyes and tight pencil grips try to write an ending to "I had fun on my vacation because…" even when they didn't go on vacation or their parents just got divorced—or they're really interested in writing about cars or they want to tell the class about their first loose tooth. I've seen thick curriculum binders filled with worksheets for students to complete and staple together, all in the name of writing.

Our students come to our classrooms wanting nothing more than to have their voices heard and to "sing their hearts out for us." Our students deserve wide-open, focused studies where they are trusted to write what they know and supported in learning what they don't yet know. It's insulting to children when our classroom instruction ignores the fact that every student we teach brings his or her own strengths and struggles, likes and dislikes to the writing table. It's our job as their teachers to make sure that we don't kill that passion for writing, that we help them fly with solid instruction, and that we celebrate when they sing.

Chapter 6

From Ordinary to Extraordinary

*Teaching and Learning About Poetry
with Primary Writers*

Poetry: Unit of Study Curriculum Map

Key Provisions (what students must have)	Big Ideas (what students should understand)	Essential Skills and Concepts (what students should be able to do)	Possible Text Supports (what students might use to support their work)	Assessment (what students will complete as documentation of growth)
• Topic choice • Daily writing time • Opportunities for writers to read the kinds of books they want to write • Demonstration, practice, teaching, and celebration during workshop period • Opportunities for writers to write a variety of genres • A purpose for writing and an audience • Support from the other authors and teachers in the classroom (students, teachers, books by published authors) • Tools necessary for writers to write and publish the kinds of pieces they envision • Time for writers to think, talk, write, and share every day	• Poets get ideas from their lives, their passions, and the books they read. • Poetry is written differently than fiction or nonfiction. Poetry doesn't have to rhyme. • Poets use interesting vocabulary, illustrations, formats, and text sizes to engage the reader and support his or her understanding. • Poets write about a variety of self-selected topics. • Poets write multiple rough drafts. • Poets revise and edit their writing. • Poets publish their writing using a variety of formats and media.	• Write in the poetic format with line breaks and white space • Use strong verbs, adjectives, and adverbs ("active" and "20/20" words) in the poems they write • Use font sizes and shapes to communicate a feeling or subject to the reader • Create rhythmic pieces using repeating words, repeating lines, alliteration, and onomatopoeia ("same-sound" and "sound-effect" words) • Create illustrations to support the writing in their poems • Use a variety of media to publish and showcase poems • Name and explain different types of poems (two voice, mask, acrostic, list, nonfiction, common theme, etc.)	• *Dirty Laundry Pile* by Paul Janeczko • *Flicker Flash* by Joan Bransfield Graham • *January Rides the Wind* by Charlotte F. Otten • *Ordinary Things* by Ralph Fletcher • *Outside the Lines* by Brad Burg • *Small Talk* by Lee Bennett Hopkins • *The Burger and The Hot Dog* by Jim Aylesworth • *What If?* by Joy Hulme • *Silver Seeds* by Paul Paolilli • *When Riddles Come Rumbling* by Rebecca Kai Dotlich • *Food Fight* by Michael J. Rosen • *Water Planet* by Ralph Fletcher • *Awakening the Heart* by Georgia Heard	• What We Know About Poetry Writing chart (pre- and poststudy) • Student work samples from beginning, middle, and end of study • Videotapes of writing share and conferences during the study • Rough and final draft work • Writing journey reflection

One morning in my first-grade classroom in Alabama, Ellie walked up to me with Ralph Fletcher's poetry book *Ordinary Things* in her hand. Ellie couldn't quite read the poems yet, but she could read the word *ordinary*. "Miss Corgill, what does *ordinary* mean?" My best six-year-old explanation to Ellie was, "It's stuff that nobody really thinks about. Stuff that's not so special—just normal. Just . . . ordinary." That answer seemed to satisfy the little writer as she bounded back to her workspace to continue writing for the day.

The primary writing workshop is the place for some pretty extraordinary things to happen, and this ordinary day was the day that I got extraordinary writing from a six-year-old. At the end of our writing time, Ellie wanted to share the poem she had written using Ralph's *Ordinary Things* as her inspiration. Here is Ellie's poem:

Stuff That Nobody Thinks About

The warm feeling.

Butterflies in your tummy.

The smell of breakfast.

The sound of pencils sharpening.

The sound of birds chirping.

Books talking.

The look of funny faces.

The taste of melting chocolate in your mouth.

The feeling of dirt under your fingernail.

The sound of music in your ear.

Stories ringing in your head.

The feeling of tears rolling down your face.

The soft feeling of your mom's hand.

The end.

This moment happened because Ellie lived in a classroom where her voice was heard and her abilities were trusted. She had the tools she needed to work: a book for inspiration, paper, pencil, and crayons. And she had the time to write and have her work read and honored.

Sometimes we as teachers forget that these elements of our teaching are just as critical as the articulation of our focus lesson or the manner in which we lead a writing conference. Our teaching and our trust in students must come together for the extraordinary to happen. Throughout this chapter you will find elements of my teaching that gently pushed my young writers forward in becoming poets, and laid the foundation for ordinary writing to become extraordinary.

Discovering the Big Ideas Through Reading and Talking

As in all other studies, before we can write poetry well, we must first read, study, and name what we notice about the poems we are reading each day. The poetry genre reading and share time begins at least three weeks before we've ended the previous writing study. We begin to read a new genre at the point when the children are in the final stages of publication—editing, rewriting, and illustrating their final drafts for the publishing celebration. For example, if our previous study was about "experience writing" (writing from what they know), the kids would be completing their final drafts while beginning to read about our new genre, poetry.

Each morning the children spend the first twenty minutes of the day reading, talking, noticing, and then sharing their observations about poetry. One habit that's essential for young children to develop is the ability to read and name their understandings of or characteristics of the genre they wish to write.

As part of our morning meeting, the children have the opportunity to name what they've noticed about the genre of poetry. As the children name what they've discovered, I chart the discovery on Post-it chart paper and write the child's name next to it. I've found that attaching specific names to what they notice encourages the entire class to make new discoveries each day and have their name and discovery put on our class chart.

Now, don't think that each day we make this incredible list with lots of discoveries. Some days we may add one or two discoveries to the list, other days we may have ten discoveries. And, yes, there are days where no one notices a thing, and that's okay. We have to give the reading time to sink into those little minds. Be patient, and in your best encouraging voice say, "Wow, we've learned so much about poetry so far. Aren't we glad we don't have to add anything new and can give that chart a rest today? Let's use what we've already learned to support us in our poetry writing today." (And then you pray that they will actually believe you and use the list of discoveries to guide their writing during workshop time.)

It's also important to remember that you can support children in their discoveries by helping them name what they are trying to say in a way that can help them as writers. It's important for students to believe that their comments are important enough to add to the chart and that their words and ideas can support the entire class of writers.

In Peter Johnston's book, *Choice Words*, he says,

> When a mother interacts with her baby, she makes something meaningful out of what the baby "says." The fact that there is not much to work with does not stop her from constructing a conversation. From "bem ba" she imputes a social intention and responds, "You want milk?" She acts as if the baby's noises are not random but are intentional discursive actions, and responds accordingly. The same is true, in a way, in the classroom. The teacher has to make something of what children say and do. (2004, 5)

When young children make comments in a typical morning poetry share, I try to help them name their discoveries in more specific writing language. I like to ask them, "Let me make sure I understand. Is this what you're trying to say?" and then I name the discovery in a way that can help the class of writers in the room. Or I might say, "So you're saying that poets sometimes . . ." Children almost always say, "Yes, that's what I was trying to say!" This is the way to still honor the talk but push children's thinking into more writerly language. The more often you use the words of writers, the more the children will begin to speak in ways that sound like writers.

Here are some actual statements from children during a first-grade poetry share in our classroom. First is what the student said, and then, in italics, is how I "make something writerly" of the child's poetry discovery. Think about these comments and how you might help the children use writing language to name their discoveries. It's this kind of conversation that gives students ownership in the share and allows them to see crafting and content possibilities for their writing.

"My dad's car makes a sound like the one in that poem!"

Writers of poetry sometimes use "sound-effect words" to make their poems come to life. (Vrroooommmmm . . . Zoooooooommmmmm!!)

"That snake poem is written like a rattlesnake curled up."

Poets sometimes write their pieces in the shape of the topic to help the reader understand the poem better. (The snake poem is written like a snake curled and ready to strike.)

"It sounds like the whale is talking in that poem!"

Sometimes poets put on a writing mask like you do at Halloween to pretend that they are another person, place, or thing.

The Whale

by Douglas Florian

Big as a street—
With fins, not feet—
I'm full of blubber,
With skin like rubber.
When I breathe out,
I spew
A spout.
I swim by the shore
And eat more and more.
I'm very, very hard to ignore. (1994)

As we read, discover, and then name our discoveries, we record this thinking on an anchor chart that hangs in the room throughout the study. And, as I've mentioned, I make sure to record each child's name beside his or her noticing or discovery. This not only builds confidence in students as "genre detectives," but also sends the message that we're building a poetry writing curriculum together. Every child has an opportunity to contribute to the writing possibilities in the room, and powerful writing comes when children believe they have the power to discover and create curriculum.

A partial list of poetry discoveries from our anchor chart follows:

What We've Noticed About Poetry from Our Reading

- ✐ Sometimes it's written in the shape of the topic or title. (Natan)
- ✐ Sometimes it's written for two or more voices. (Dasha)
- ✐ The authors use short phrases or words to create the poem. (Reede)
- ✐ There is lots of white space around the poem. The words don't cover the entire page. (Nicholas)

- It can be very short, medium-sized, or very long. (Max)

- Poets sometimes use colors or font sizes/types to help the reader understand. (Scott)

- Poets use capitalization and punctuation differently than fiction and nonfiction writers. There may not be any capital letters or punctuation in the entire poem. (Sindy)

- Poetry doesn't have to rhyme. (Caitlin)

- Poets use lots of "active" words to bring the poem to life. (Erin)

- Poems sometimes have illustrations. (Abigail)

Poetry Bags

After the children begin to notice common elements emerging in the books they read each morning, we start to make "poetry bags." or mentor text sets, for the children to use during writing workshop. I use the same bags for these mentor text sets as I do for each student's individual reading bag for reading workshop.

As a class we name the common element or characteristic we see in all the books, and then all those books are added to one bag. Each year the names for the kinds of poetry bags may be a bit different, depending on what makes sense to a particular group of students. Here are some examples of types of poetry bags we've created in previous poetry units.

Two-Voice Poems

These are books with poems that are written for two voices to read aloud. These kinds of books are great for partner reading, and are great to use in a poetry reader's theater to help the children practice their fluency and expression when reading aloud. Mary Ann Hoberman's *You Read to Me and I'll Read to You* is always a favorite of my primary readers and writers. The children also love the fact that the voices are distinguished by color in the book. For example, one child will read all the words written in blue, and the other child will read the words written in red. They also recognize that sometimes a color signifies that that part should be read together. Throughout our poetry study I see variations of this style in the children's writing—they've written parts of their poem in one color and another part in a different color, and they ask a friend to read along with them when they share at the end of the workshop period.

Mask Poems

I learned the term *mask* poem from JoAnn Portalupi and Ralph Fletcher in their book *Nonfiction Craft Lessons* (2001), and it makes so much sense to young writers. I use the analogy of wearing a mask at Halloween to pretend you're something else. Writers are a lot like kids at Halloween. To entertain their readers, they sometimes put on a mask of another person, place, or thing. *Dirty Laundry Pile*, poems selected by Paul Janeczko, never fails as one of the class's favorite mask poem books. "The Vacuum Cleaner's Revenge" is a favorite where poet Patricia Hubbell writes from the perspective of the vacuum cleaner: "I crunch, I munch, I zoom, I roar… I clatter clack across the floor." Here are two examples of mask poems by former second graders Erin and Caitlin.

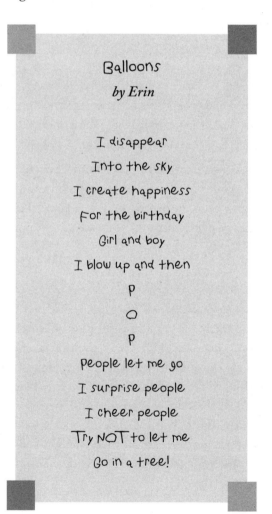

Balloons
by Erin

I disappear
Into the sky
I create happiness
For the birthday
Girl and boy
I blow up and then
P
O
P
People let me go
I surprise people
I cheer people
Try NOT to let me
Go in a tree!

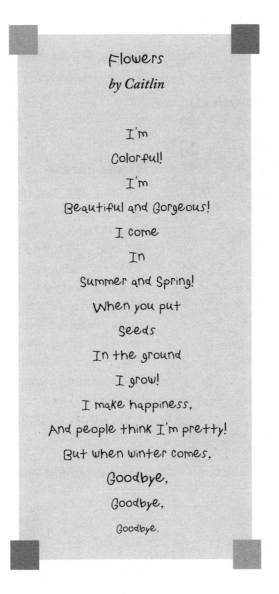

Flowers
by Caitlin

I'm
Colorful!
I'm
Beautiful and Gorgeous!
I come
In
Summer and Spring!
When you put
Seeds
In the ground
I grow!
I make happiness,
And people think I'm pretty!
But when winter comes,
Goodbye,
Goodbye,
Goodbye.

Shape and Pattern Poems

Young children find this type of poem intriguing and fun to both read and write. Two of our favorite books with poems written in the shape of the topic of the poem are *Flicker Flash* by Joan Bransfield Graham and *Outside the Lines* by Brad Burg. In *Flicker Flash* a poem called "Lightning Bolt" about Ben Franklin discovering electricity is written in the shape of a lightning bolt coming from the sky. You can also find a poem about a campfire with words flickering like flames on the page. A poem about the sun is circular and positioned on the page right outside a window. Dugagjin Idrizaj, one of my former second graders, wrote a poem called "Superman

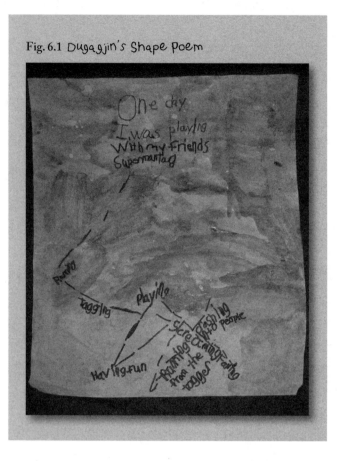

Fig. 6.1 Dugagjin's Shape Poem

Tag" that was inspired by the poem "Soccer" from *Outside the Lines.* (See Figure 6.1.) Both Dugagjin and Brad Burg used dashes and dotted lines to connect words like *Run, Kick It, Having Fun, Playing, I've GOT It,* and *GOAL.*

Riddle Poems

Rebecca Kai Dotlich would be happy to know that the pages of our classroom copy of her book *When Riddles Come Rumbling* are worn and torn and full of first-grade fingerprints. This past year, my students loved this poetry book and worked to emulate the poems they read each day. In this book Dotlich keeps the reader guessing till the end of each poem and uses the illustrations to give away the subject. Riddle poems showed up in almost every child's writing folder. (And as we read each day, the children noticed that these riddle poems in this particular book were also mask poems, as Dotlich wrote them from the voice of her subject.) Take a look at this riddle poem about bees by first grader Haley:

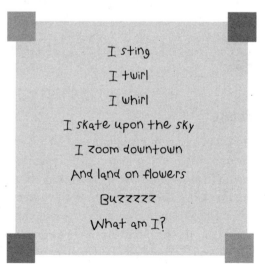

Nonfiction Poems

Judy Sierra's *Antarctic Antics* was the impetus for a discussion about poems that "teach us stuff." As we read this book together and as children gravitated toward it during morning genre reading, we learned lots of facts about penguins *and* learned lots about the craft of poetry. From that moment on, many children began writing what we called teaching poems or nonfiction poems. These poems were a lot like the nonfiction books we were reading but were written in poetry form. Take a look at this poem about fish by Daniel, a former second grader:

FINS
FLAP
GILLS
BREATHE
THEIR MOUTHS GO
"Blobbb."
LAY
EGGS
HATCH
EGGS
IT
STARTS
ALL
OVER
AGAIN!

From Daniel we learn basic facts about fish—that they have fins and breathe with gills, they lay eggs, and the cycle of life begins again! Daniel even described the sound he imagines their mouths to make: "Blobbb"!

Photographic Poems

These poetry books are filled with photographs rather than sketched or painted illustrations. Paul Janeczko's book *Stone Bench in an Empty Park* is an excellent example for the children as it gives life to the poet's words with photos. Children have the option of purchasing a disposable camera along with the regular school supplies so that they may use it to take pictures that support the writing work they're doing, rather than simply illustrating that work. I've also ventured through the city taking shots of landmarks or city scenes for the children to choose from to inspire poetry writing. Jessica and Maya, both former second graders, used pictures I had taken of a parking meter and garbage outside a building on trash day. Using the mask perspective once again, these girls were inspired by photos of a city they knew so well.

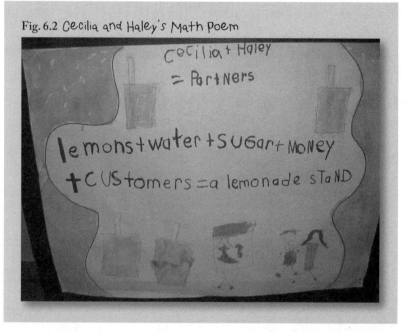

Fig. 6.2 Cecilia and Haley's Math Poem

Math Poems

The "math poem" idea came from one book that I picked up in a bookstore a few years back. Betsy Franco's *Mathematickles!* gave me a completely different formatting idea to share with students: poems written as math equations. Why not use our knowledge of how math equations are typically written and replace the numbers with words. In Figures 6.2 and 6.3, you'll find examples of math poems my first graders wrote this year.

Fig. 6.3 Sindy and Christian's Math Poem

Acrostic Poems

In an acrostic poem, the first letter of each line, when read together, make up a word. This word is typically the title or the subject of the poem. Paul Paolilli's book *Silver Seeds* is one of my favorite examples of poetry written in acrostic form.

As you have probably noticed by now, the poetry we read and use as models tends to be heavily free verse. Not a lot of rhyming poems in the mix. Why? My number one reason: Have you ever read poems by a six-year-old who tries to rhyme and make sense at the same time? Dreadful. And when I try to confer with students about their rhyming attempt, all sense of ownership goes out the window. I find this immediate need to take over and make it better—fast!

It's my "professional primary opinion" that young children's talent and ability to make the ordinary seem extraordinary come so much more naturally when they aren't trying to be Shel Silverstein, Jack Prelutsky, or Dr. Seuss. I certainly respect these authors for the type of writing they do, but this kind of rhyming work seems to stifle instead of free my young writers. Children at this age don't have the broad vocabulary to draw from when deciding on appropriate and meaningful rhyming words for their text, and it's difficult to both rhyme and communicate a clear message to the reader. Plus, as their teacher, I am drawn to and inspired by poems that don't rhyme, and in order to teach something well, I have to, at the very least, be passionate about what I'm teaching and believe that young children can learn to do what we're studying very well.

Idea Development and Crafting

Starting the Poetry Process

How do poems like the ones I've shared come to life? How does it happen? Idea development first starts with reading. Lots of reading and talking and naming possible topics. One of the ways I begin to help children develop ideas for poetry is to help them think like an artist or an illustrator. Children in the primary grades naturally gravitate to drawing and coloring, and much of their "written" work is in the form of pictures. During our read-aloud time, I ask the children to visualize poems I read, and then illustrate and color their visualizations on poetry support sheets. (See Figures 6.4 and 6.5 for examples. A blank visualization support sheet is provided in Appendix C.) From these illustrations comes lots of talk about what each writer/listener saw as I was reading a particular poem. This talk time is an opportunity for describing, naming, and explaining the

Fig. 6.4 Example of a Poetry Support Sheet

Jacob
Poetry Support Sheet
Good writers sometimes start a rough draft with a visualization instead of with words. (They illustrate poetry before writing it.)

A Rough Draft of My Visualization

Fig. 6.5 Example of a Poetry Support Sheet

Emma

Poetry Support Sheet
Good writers sometimes start a rough draft
with a visualization instead of with words.
(They illustrate poetry before writing it.)

A Rough Draft of My Visualization

Dictionary of
A,B,Cs and 1,2,3s

illustrations the children have completed. As a class we use the visualization support sheet several times in reading poetry aloud, and then we talk about the similarities and differences in the poetry. Then, as children are beginning to write their first poems, some children choose to "draw" their first poem and talk to me about the illustration instead of writing it. Many times their illustrations spark more ideas than just sitting and thinking about a topic (or even talking with me in a conference).

I also provide support sheets that give the children a place to record topic ideas as they read or work in writing time during the day. These support sheets stay in the students' rough draft folders until the end of the study, when they become a part of their poetry writing journey folder.

Organization and Design

It's important for primary students to begin to recognize that poetry, fiction, and nonfiction texts look differently from one another—that the words and illustrations are placed differently on the page. In my time as a primary teacher, I've found that young children usually have had lots more experience reading (and being read to) with fiction and nonfiction texts. Equally noticeable is the kind of writing they produce. When they write from their own experiences, it usually comes in the form of a story that fills the page with approximated spelling, illustrations, and lots of staples to make their book. A poetry study in the primary grades is the perfect opportunity to expand the writing knowledge of five-, six-, and seven-year-olds and help them to see how different genres are organized and designed.

As we read poetry each day, the children begin to notice that there are fewer words on a page. There's a lot of blank, white space around the poem. Some poems have only a few words or a few lines. Others are written in the shape of the topic or in an acrostic form. Some words show up in boldfaced print while others are written in fancy fonts or large and small sizes, to help convey meaning to the reader.

When helping the children organize and design their poems, I usually focus on four elements: white space, font sizes, shape of poem, and line breaks. Children learn quickly that writers use font sizes and types to convey a particular meaning in a poem. Boldface words in all capital letters usually signify excitement or surprise, or let the reader know that this word should be read in a strong, loud voice. On the other hand, words can show meaning as the size changes through the poem. In Caitlin's poem about flowers, the second grader shows the reader what happens to a flower in winter, changing the size of the word *goodbye* to signify that the flower is dying or won't be in bloom for the winter months ahead.

Goodbye,

Goodbye,

Goodbye.

When the children are learning about line breaks and white space in poetry and how this genre looks different than fiction and nonfiction, I usually engage them in several lessons using poems on a pocket chart. I write the poem on sentence strips and cut the poem apart into each individual word. It's usually a poem we've read aloud or one that's a favorite of the class. For this kind of lesson, I deliberately place the words on the pocket chart to read like fiction. Our job in the lesson is to then reorganize the poem so that it both looks and sounds like poetry when it's read aloud. The children negotiate the placement of the words, and we reread as we go through each line. It reinforces the idea that poets make deliberate choices about the placement of their words on a page, so that the poem reads in a musical, logical, and poetic way. I engage children in several lessons like this one with different poems each time, and then I create a place in the room where these poems are housed in large zippered plastic bags (with a copy of the original poem inside). During morning genre-reading time, the children can use these poems and explore ways to place the words and read the poem aloud at share time.

Once children have had experience as a whole class with this exercise, I then give them a support sheet to try on their own (much like what we've done as a whole class in a focus lesson). See Sydney's support sheet in Figure 6.6.

Fig. 6.6 Sydney's Support Sheet

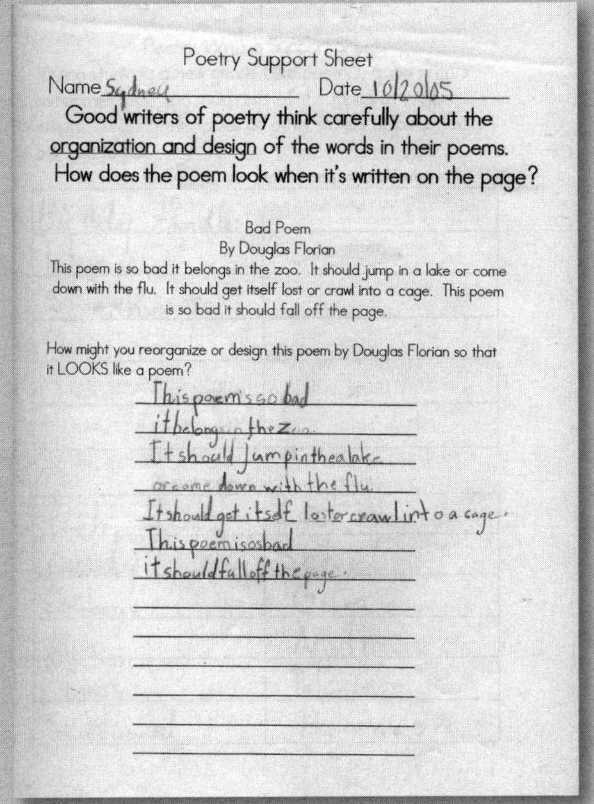

Poetry Support Sheet

Name Sydney   Date 10/20/05

Good writers of poetry think carefully about the organization and design of the words in their poems. How does the poem look when it's written on the page?

Bad Poem
By Douglas Florian

This poem is so bad it belongs in the zoo. It should jump in a lake or come down with the flu. It should get itself lost or crawl into a cage. This poem is so bad it should fall off the page.

How might you reorganize or design this poem by Douglas Florian so that it LOOKS like a poem?

This poem's so bad
it belongs in the zoo.
It should jump in the lake
or come down with the flu.
It should get itself lost or crawl into a cage.
This poem is so bad
it should fall off the page.

Fig. 6.7 Ryan Arranges His Poem

When students are writing their own poems in workshop time, I provide the poetry puzzle paper seen on the right-hand side of Figure 6.7 to help students arrange the words on the page before writing a final draft. This sheet is for children who need support in their work with line breaks and how to organize their poem on the page. (A blank poetry puzzle support sheet is provided in Appendix C.) Children put their rough draft alongside the poetry puzzle paper and then write each word from the rough draft in a separate box. Then, when they've written the entire rough draft on the poetry puzzle paper, they cut out each word. Now the entire poem is like a puzzle, ready to be placed, arranged, and rearranged in a way that both looks and sounds like poetry. Once they have organized their poems, they are then ready to write the final draft. Figure 6.7 shows Ryan working to arrange his poem.

Word Choice and Voice

As I watched TV from across the living room last night, the channels looked a bit fuzzy. This morning I looked out my window, and the tree off my balcony was one big green blur rather than lots of individual leaves growing on the giant oak. My friend and I went to the movies last week, and I needed to sit in the first few rows at the movie theater so I could enjoy the film without squinting for two hours and leaving the theater with a headache. Yep. It's time for new glasses and contacts. When I go to the eye doctor to get a new pair of glasses or contacts, it's my expectation that the doctor will work to tweak my prescription so that I will leave the office with 20/20 vision. The television channels will then be crisp, colors of leaves will be sharp, and characters brought to life on the big screen will be perfectly clear as I sit in the back row of the theater.

I share this story with my young writers as we begin to explore the language of poetry and specific word choices of poets. I explain to the kids that writers are sometimes a lot like eye doctors. Poets, like ophthalmologists, work to give their readers, their clients, a clear, crisp, 20/20 vision as they create and craft a piece of writing. A poet is also like an artist, painting a picture in the mind of the reader. In years past I've covered the tables in our classroom with butcher paper as an invitation for children to write interesting words or phrases from the books they're reading. This year the bathroom door in the classroom was covered with "20/20," "active," "same-sound," and "sound-effect" words (also known as adjectives, adverbs, and verbs, alliteration, and onomatopoeia to my first graders). However, the descriptions *20/20*, *active*, *sound-effect*, and *same-sound* made a lot more sense to my six-year-olds, but what's very cool is that by the time the children start to learn about adjectives, adverbs, and verbs or alliteration and onomatopoeia in the older grades, they will have already had lots of experience using these types of words in their writing. I believe in giving children experience with all kinds of language, but also giving them developmentally appropriate ways to use that new knowledge. My friend Sharon Taberski introduced me to the book *Bringing Words to Life*, by Beck, McKeown, and Kucan, and this book about robust vocabulary instruction has supported my work in helping young writers become aware of, explore, and use language in interesting ways. I provide support sheets like the one in Figure 6.8 to help students write poetry that gives the reader a 20/20 image and to help them paint pictures with their words. (See Appendix C for a blank 20/20 words support sheet.)

Fig. 6.8 20/20 Words vs. Blurry Words: Emma's Support Sheet

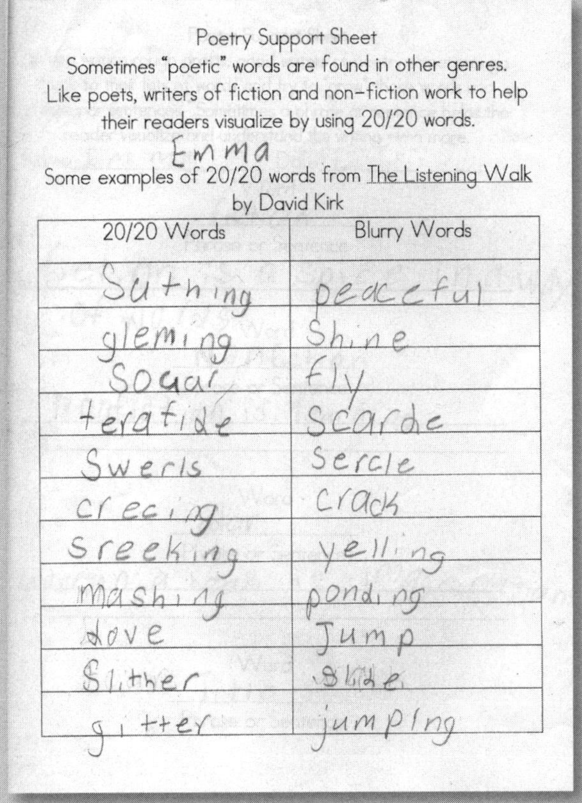

Poetry Support Sheet
Sometimes "poetic" words are found in other genres.
Like poets, writers of fiction and non-fiction work to help their readers visualize by using 20/20 words.
Emma
Some examples of 20/20 words from The Listening Walk by David Kirk

20/20 Words	Blurry Words
Suthing	peaceful
gleming	Shine
Soaar	fly
terafide	scarde
Swerls	sercle
crecing	crack
sreeking	yelling
mashing	ponding
dove	Jump
Slither	slide
gitter	jumping

Noah used his knowledge of same-sound words to write a nonfiction poem about birds during our study of the birds of Central Park in second grade.

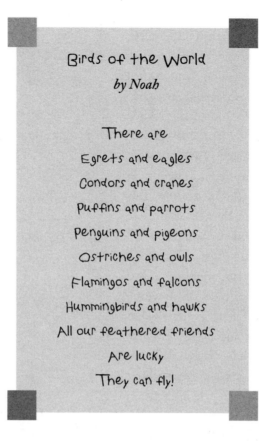

Birds of the World
by Noah

There are
Egrets and eagles
Condors and cranes
Puffins and parrots
Penguins and pigeons
Ostriches and owls
Flamingos and falcons
Hummingbirds and hawks
All our feathered friends
Are lucky
They can fly!

Former second grader Reede wrote a poem about New York City and filled it with active words, same-sound words, and sound-effect words to give her readers a clear image of life in the city.

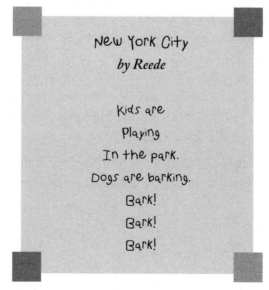

New York City
by Reede

Kids are
Playing
In the park.
Dogs are barking.
Bark!
Bark!
Bark!

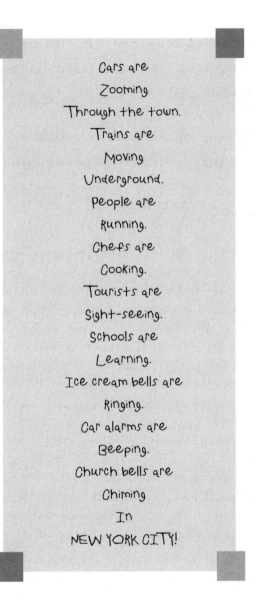

Cars are
Zooming
Through the town.
Trains are
Moving
Underground.
People are
Running.
Chefs are
Cooking.
Tourists are
Sight-seeing.
Schools are
Learning.
Ice cream bells are
Ringing.
Car alarms are
Beeping.
Church bells are
Chiming
In
NEW YORK CITY!

A Typical Day During Our Poetry Study

What does our writing workshop time look like during a poetry study? What does it sound like? How is the workshop period organized?

First of all, I can guarantee that we'll be writing every day and that the workshop period will last at least one hour. During that hour, you will most typically find us first gathering as a class on the rug to begin the workshop together. This beginning workshop time usually lasts around ten minutes. In this ten-minute block of time you will find us doing one of the following:

- Participating in a new focus lesson on one aspect of poetry
- Reviewing a previous lesson from the previous day or days before
- Sharing a piece of children's writing that supports the lesson or work we've been doing in genre share
- Reading and discussing a poem and its characteristics
- Reviewing workshop routines or ways to use materials
- Checking the status of the class to find out what each child is working on or where he or she is in the process

You will notice from this list that not every beginning of writing workshop begins with a focus lesson on crafting, idea generating, revising, or editing. Although many days are devoted to those elements, I've given myself permission to broaden the idea of what it means to teach a lesson at the beginning of the workshop period. What's most important to me is that the way we start the workshop should set the tone for the rest of that hour block of time, and a new focus lesson isn't always the best way to begin. Sometimes the kids just need extra time to process what we've learned the day before. Sometimes it's important to share a poem we all love and talk about what we notice. Sometimes I need to make sure I'm on target and know where all children are in their process so that I can provide extra support to those children who might be stuck in their writing work. Sometimes it's important to review routines or redefine the expectations for the day. Understand that all this work is teaching children how to be better poets, focused writers and readers, and more accountable students. That's what we want: children who are eager to start their writing work for the day, are not overwhelmed by a shove-it-down-their-throats curriculum, and are engaged in the writing process from beginning to end.

The next part of the workshop period is the work and practice time, the time for children to think, write, and talk about their writing either with classmates or with me in individual conferences or guided writing groups. This part of the workshop lasts around forty minutes—less or more time depending on the time of year. This writing time is obviously much shorter at the beginning of the year, when we're just practicing routines, developing writing stamina, and learning how to focus our attention for a sustained amount of time. As the year goes on and the children grow, this writing time grows along with the children.

At the end of the workshop, the children gather to share their work the last ten to fifteen minutes of the period. Typically, children who share are the ones I've had individual conferences with that particular day. These children share their poetry teaching points and teach the class what they learned. This is a great way for me to assess whether or not the child internalized my teaching and used that conference to support his or her writing work that day. It's also a great way to manage who shares on what day and why they get to share. I've found that everyone wants to share, and this is a logical and fair way to make sure that each child's voice is equally heard and respected.

I've found that it works better to have cleanup time after the share. That way the children have time to move from share on the rug, clean the room, and return all materials to their proper places—as well as having time to move around again before settling in on the rug for the next workshop period.

If you visited my classroom at the *beginning* of our poetry study, you might find students doing the following:

1. Making lists of possible poetry topics

2. Using our genre-share chart to get ideas for their rough drafts

3. Writing or illustrating rough drafts

4. Conferring with me about their work

5. Finding appropriate tools (crayons, markers, colored pencils, poetry paper) for their work for the day

6. Talking with classmates about their writing work

7. Sharing what they've written in share time and teaching the class what they learned in their individual conferences with me

If you visited my classroom in the *middle* of our poetry study, you might find students doing the following:

1. Conferring with me about their multiple drafts or final choices for publication

2. Rereading poetry and checking for appropriate line breaks so that their writing both looks and sounds like poetry

3. Correcting as many spelling errors as possible (using words in the room, their spelling dictionaries, and help from friends)

4. Revising by replacing blah words, as we call them, with active and 20/20 words.

5. Illustrating their poetry

6. Sharing their pieces with classmates and teaching the class goals from independent conferences

If you visited my classroom at the *end* of our poetry study, you might find students doing the following:

1. Writing or illustrating their final draft poems

2. Gathering all rough drafts and poetry support sheets from their rough draft folders to be placed in their poetry writing journey folders

3. Completing their poetry writing reflections to go in their poetry writing journey folders

4. Conferring with me about last-minute details, spelling corrections, additions to their pieces or reflections

5. Cutting, pasting, painting, writing, outlining, mounting, organizing, talking, laughing, preparing for the publishing celebration

Reflecting on Our Work and Learning

A few days before each publishing celebration, I ask the children to complete a "poetry writing journey reflection." This reflection is a great way to assess what children have learned during the study, what lessons supported their work, what books inspired their writing, and what their feelings are about the writing that was produced and published. (A blank writing journey form for the poetry study is provided in Appendix C.) From Natan's reflection (Figure 6.9) I learn about his journey as a second-grade poet. As his teacher, I learn from Natan that passion and knowledge about a subject can be the root of a powerful writing project:

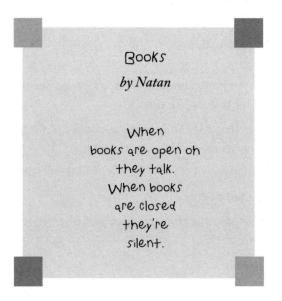

Books

by Natan

When
books are open oh
they talk.
When books
are closed
they're
silent.

But when they're open
they're alive.
Can you please
read me
again?
I'll bring you
far away.
So open me.
Go anywhere.
On the shore
across the sea.
Go anywhere.
Go in the
middle of an
apple tree.
Go anywhere.
Swing to poetry
you might find
rhymes.
Go anywhere.
Climb to nonfiction.
You'll find facts.
Go anywhere.
Walk to fiction.
You'll get ideas.
Go anywhere.
I told you.
Go anywhere.
Go anywhere
To places you've
never heard of.
Go anywhere.
Say yes to books.
Go anywhere.
You'll find a friend.
So.
Go anywhere.
In books.

Fig. 6.9a Natan's Poetry Writing Journey Reflection

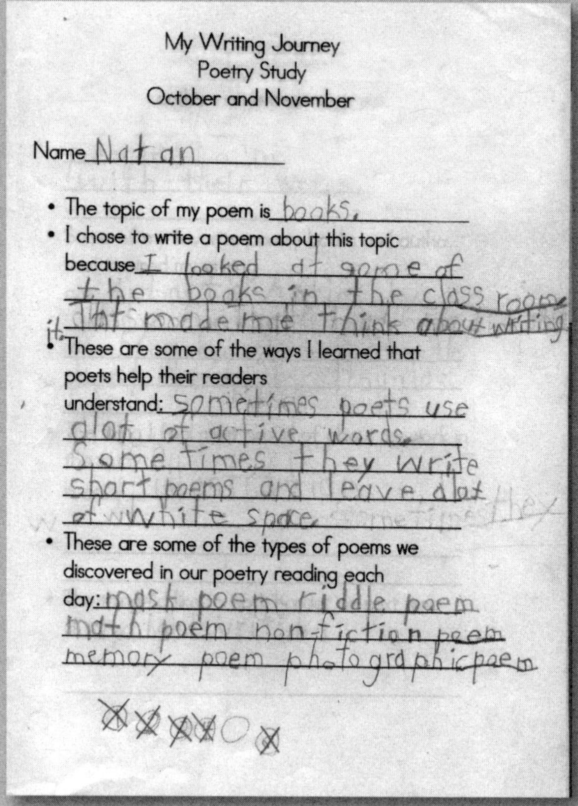

My Writing Journey
Poetry Study
October and November

Name Natan

- The topic of my poem is books,
- I chose to write a poem about this topic because I looked at some of the books in the class room it. That made me think about writing
- These are some of the ways I learned that poets help their readers understand: Sometimes poets use a lot of active words. Sometimes they write short poems and leave a lot of white space. sometimes they
- These are some of the types of poems we discovered in our poetry reading each day: mask poem riddle poem math poem non-fiction poem memory poem photographic poem

Fig. 6.9b

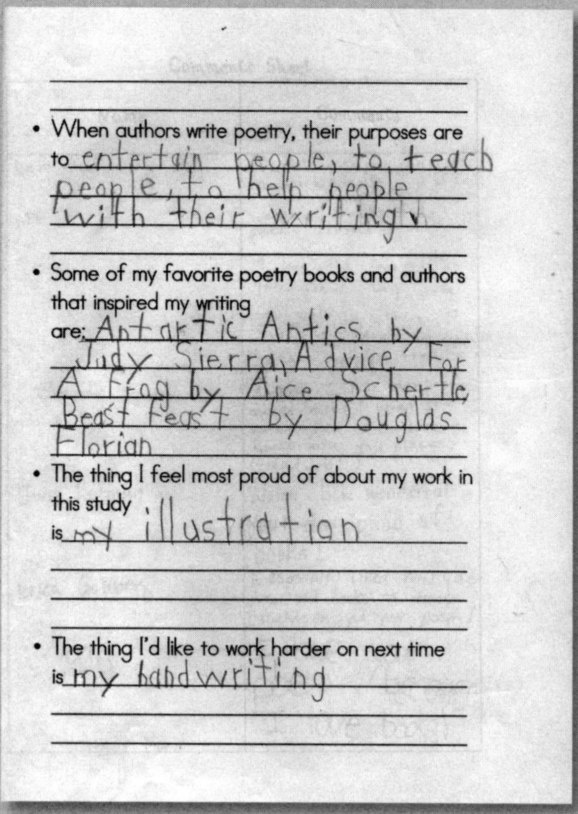

- When authors write poetry, their purposes are to entertain people, to teach people, to help people with their writing.
- Some of my favorite poetry books and authors that inspired my writing are: Antarctic Antics by Judy Sierra, Advice For A Frog by Alice Schertle Beast Feast by Douglas Florian
- The thing I feel most proud of about my work in this study is my illustration
- The thing I'd like to work harder on next time is my handwriting

Natan's love for reading inspired his work, and in that work he beautifully communicated how books can take us places. Natan helped the reader see books through new eyes. He shows beyond-his-years knowledge of how to use repetition in powerful ways. Photographs of favorite book covers grace the sides of his poem, adding beauty, detail, and even more ownership to the piece. He's clearly aware of the purposes for writing poetry and is able to articulate specific crafting techniques and vocabulary that supports and enhances a poet's writing. Natan not only is aware of his passions as a writer, but he has knowledge of the purposes for reading and writing poetry (to entertain readers and to teach people). He also has several favorite mentor texts that supported and inspired his work. This knowledge of books and other authors as mentors for his work signals that Natan understands that writing isn't the isolated development of a skill or a "one-man show" in our classroom, that we use all our resources to get ideas and sustain our writing work over the weeks and months in a study. Our writing process is a community effort, and each child is aware of and part of the work of his or her classmates. Natan is a goal-oriented and planful student. These traits speak loudly in his reflection as he demonstrates an understanding of the ongoing process of writing in our classroom and in his world. He feels proud of his illustration and is planning to work harder on his handwriting in his next writing project.

So much of Natan's learning is captured in his published piece, but the reflection takes his learning as a poet one step further. The reflection allows this young writer to think back from the beginning of our study of poetry and name significant events, lessons and mentor texts that supported his work, possibilities and purposes for writing poetry, successes as a writer, and plans for reaching new goals and pursuing future writing projects. Thinking back pushes a young writer forward, and Natan taught me lots about his growth forward as a writer of poetry.

Studying poetry gives children a nonthreatening way to write powerfully without being overwhelmed by the complexity and difficulty of producing pages and pages of text for a reader to comprehend. For this reason, I teach poetry as one of the first studies of the year. I teach poetry because I love it, but also because it gives young children an opportunity for instant success as writers. This kind of writing is typically short and lends itself to interesting formats and designs, playful use of punctuation and language, opportunities to communicate with less text, and easy ways to publish and showcase the writing and illustrating work. Notebook entries, slices of conversation, and bits and pieces of stories and rough draft work can become beautifully written, well-crafted, powerful poetry. Help your young writers see the power and the purpose in poetry, writing extraordinarily from the ordinary—from the "stuff that nobody thinks about."

Primary writers at work in our classroom.

The small-group writing area of the classroom.

The writing materials area.

First graders proudly showcasing their poetry posters.

Cecilia's published picture book.

Five Puppies Taking A Chance

Where are the Buddies?

I Don't know!

Written and Illustrated by Cecilia Had

Buddies are Born

There was a dog that had puppies. She was very happy! She named her pups Dede, Rose, Shimmer, Gorgerie and Mina.

Buddies are Born

Then there was there Aunt Tasha! We knew she would come to see the new puppies! She was carrying a bouquet of roses for Mom.

---

yay for aunt Tasha! and she was carrying a present! Who could it be for? Us? Mina was drama queen and beauty expert like

---

her mom. Shimmer skateboards, G. roller blades, Dede meditats. Unfortunatly mom and Dad ran away after the puppies were born! Mom! Dad!, bit

But it was too late! They were gone! How could they leave us now? The puppies took a chance and decided to live in another puppy homes.

They got up and stared to think. Then started to walk. They walked and walked and walked....

Theyfound 5 new homes with new parents.

Mina went to a home with a drama queen beauty expert. Rose went to an athletic family. Dede went to a family that parctices yoga. Georgerie went to a rollerderby expert family

And they all lived Happily ever after.

About The Author

Cecilia Hail is 6!? She has written alot of books. A book called Fun On The Run is by me. I have written poetry. I love dogs. But hatealotofcats but 2 I love. I wrote this Book because I Love DOGS! 4 years I have been author I will write poetry next. Bye!

A bulletin board of poetry discoveries from our reading-for-writing share time.

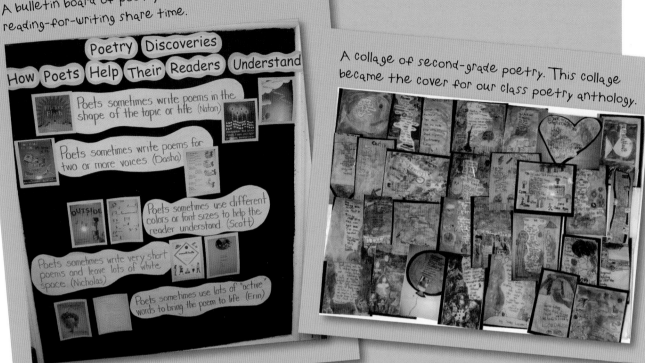

A collage of second-grade poetry. This collage became the cover for our class poetry anthology.

Our published Did You Know...? Bubbles.

Mark's procedural writing piece, "How to Be a Secret Agent."

Chapter 7

Inquiring Minds Want to Know

*Teaching and Learning About Nonfiction
with Primary Writers*

Nonfiction: Unit of Study Curriculum Map

Key Provisions (what students must have)	Big Ideas (what students should understand)	Essential Skills and Concepts (what students should be able to do)	Possible Text Supports (what students might use to support their work)	Assessments (what students will complete as documentation of growth)
• Topic choice • Daily writing time • Opportunities for writers to read the kinds of books they want to write • Demonstration, practice, teaching, and celebration during workshop period • Opportunities for writers to write a variety of genres • A purpose for writing and an audience • Support from the other authors and teachers in the classroom (students, teachers, books by published authors) • Tools necessary for writers to write and publish the kinds of pieces they envision • Time for writers to think, talk, write, and share every day	• Writers can build background knowledge by reading nonfiction. • Writers can organize their writing using specific nonfiction features. • Writers can teach their readers through nonfiction writing. • Writers can engage their readers by using interesting titles, clear formats, supporting illustrations, and well-crafted writing. • Writers can publish their nonfiction writing in a variety of ways.	• Read expository and procedural writing to develop knowledge about a subject • Become familiar with the features of nonfiction and how they support the reader's understanding • Use nonfiction features in writing to support the reader's understanding of the text • Write dash facts from reading and research so that information isn't copied directly from the text • Organize information into subcategories, subheadings, or steps • Write with voice and personality • Publish nonfiction writing about a specific topic	• *Bat Loves the Night* by Nicola Davies • *Ice Bear* by Nicola Davies • *What Do You Do With a Tail Like This?* by Steve Jenkins • *Atlantic* by G. Brian Karas • *Are You a Butterfly?* by Judy Allen • DK Look Closer series • Lodestar See How They Grow series • *Penguins Are Waterbirds* by Sharon Taberski • Heinemann Read and Learn series • *Look to the North: A Wolf Pup Diary* by Jean Craighead George • *It's a Frog's Life* by Steve Parker • *Diary of a Worm* by Doreen Cronin	• What We Know About Nonfiction Writing chart (pre- and poststudy) • Student work samples from beginning, middle, and end of study • Videotapes of writing share and conferences during the study • Rough and final draft work • Writing journey reflection • Published piece

> *It is in fact nothing short of a miracle that the modern methods of instruction have not yet entirely strangled the holy curiosity of inquiry; for this delicate little plant, aside from stimulation, stands mainly in need of freedom; without this it goes to wrack and ruin without fail.*
>
> —Albert Einstein

My sister and brother-in-law love it when I visit for the weekend, because I'm a morning person just like their five-year-old son, Jack. And Aunt Ann Marie makes it possible for his mom and dad to arise after the sun. These wake-up calls from Jack before the crack of dawn usually involve invented activities like "Guess the Instrument" or "I'm Thinking of an Animal," games where we make up musical or animal riddles and Jack or I guess the instrument or animal based on the characteristics given. You might also find me being directed to "Draw Me a Picture of a," where Jack names his topic, and I find myself working hard to live up to his illustrating expectations. Jack loves to sing, visit the pet store and the zoo, and make pictures for Mommy to hang on the refrigerator. He wants to be a conductor, a zookeeper, and a painter when he grows up.

Jack's fascination with these topics is honored. His family regularly visits the bookstore and the library, and he comes home with books about his interests. Jack's five, and he can't read yet, but he's been read to in the womb, in the high chair, and in the laps of the people who love him. Thousands of hours of read-aloud time. His family and friends ask questions about animals, instruments, and art, and Jack is quick to ask just as many questions and be persistent in getting an answer. He talks and is talked to. His little voice is heard and respected. Visits to the zoo in Anchorage, the Bronx, and Birmingham bring his reading to life. A trip with his preschool teacher to hear the symphony and Mommy-and-me art classes make those interests all the more relevant. Jack doesn't know it, but he has already received some of the greatest gifts a child could want or need, and he's not even in kindergarten.

I want the same for every child I teach. I want the students in my class to have the opportunity for their little "inquiring minds to know." I want them to read, and think, and question, and wonder—and then have the freedom to write about those questions, wonderings, and new knowledge. The world around us is fascinating and fabulous, and young children are naturally curious about it all. Hence, a nonfiction writing study to help my students come to know that their lives are nonfiction and writers of nonfiction learn and grow through their interests.

So many possibilities exist when teaching nonfiction, and it's virtually impossible to explore all avenues unless you have the privilege of keeping your same students through their entire elementary career. So give yourself permission to choose from the wide range of possibilities and go with your gut, and your students' abilities and interests, and respect the time you have set aside for this study in your curriculum calendar.

Over the years with my primary students, I have chosen two separate and distinct studies under the umbrella of nonfiction that would give students a wide range of opportunities in exploring topics of interest to them. Some years I have focused on only one nonfiction study, while in other years, my students and I have explored more than one type of nonfiction writing.

Our study of nonfiction in writing workshop supports the content-area curriculum research and projects and helps students write about our science and social studies learning. Let me be clear that our content-area (science and social studies) writing work is *always separate* from the writing workshop time in our classroom. I believe that when content curriculum engulfs the writing workshop, student choice is limited and the content curriculum limits opportunities for studying actual writing craft, features, and techniques. That's why our work in a nonfiction writing genre *supports and enhances* but doesn't take the place of the content curriculum requirements and vice versa.

In our nonfiction genre studies, we've pursued:

- Informational writing that explains or gives specific facts about a topic using nonfiction features as a primary focus. In our "Features Focus" writing study, the children wrote and published survey posters, giving a wide range of information about a topic through the use of nonfiction features found in the texts we read. The class name for these round posters became "Did You Know…? Bubbles." (See the example in Figure 7.1 and see Appendix D for a nonfiction Did You Know…? Bubble titles support sheet.)

Fig. 7.1 Example of a Did You Know…? Bubble

- Informational writing that gives a sequence or a method for the reader to follow (procedural or advice writing). In this procedural writing study, the children produced short "how-to" books.

Our writing work in these two studies allowed us to later pursue content-area projects where the children wrote and published literary nonfiction picture books to go along with classroom museum exhibits about the birds of New York City.

Essential Skills and Concepts

Our work in a study grows out of (1) what I believe about writing and understand as best practice in writing instruction and (2) what I believe young children can accomplish as writers. In our study of nonfiction, we dig deeply into our writing and reading work—studying a variety of texts and ways to go about writing information we know and have learned. This is usually the longest genre study of the year and it encompasses several publications. We generally work through some type of study under the umbrella of nonfiction from January through April of the school year.

I use the essential skills and concepts from the curriculum map to guide our focus lessons, conferences, reading discovery times, and writing share times. It's these skills, concepts, and expectations for my young writers that provide a frame for my teaching and fuel for the study of nonfiction.

The sections that follow each focus on a different essential skill or concept include details on the ways we brought those concepts and skills to life in the classroom in both our nonfiction features study and in our procedural writing. Be aware that these two studies were separate four- to five-week writing units, but the overarching skills and concepts were the same. I will explain how each essential skill or concept specifically related to the nonfiction study we were pursuing. At the end of this chapter is a chart that can be used as a guide for conferences during a nonfiction study.

I want my students to read multiple texts and become familiar with the features of nonfiction and how those features support the reader's understanding. We will also read to develop knowledge about topic, craft, and organization in the nonfiction genre.

Just as in all other studies, the children and I spend weeks (which quickly turn into months) reading, talking, and naming our discoveries about the nonfiction texts we read. I intentionally pull books from the classroom library that will support our studies of nonfiction features, procedural/advice writing, and literary nonfiction. These books will be the cornerstones of our conversations about writing over the next few months, and the children will come to know these texts well.

For example, I gather picture books written in an enumerative structure, one that has general information about a topic and is typically followed by information under subheadings or subtopics. I also select books written in a narrative structure, which usually provide examples of interesting introductions and writing from multiple points of view with "voice and personality"—which simply means ways to craft a factual text with interesting language, questions, or structures. I also include examples of procedural or advice writing, so that the children can get a sense of how authors teach or advise their readers about a topic.

We then chart our discoveries over the days, weeks, and months and include the names of the texts these discoveries came from as well as the child's name who discovered a particular nonfiction characteristic. Peter Johnston calls this type of work in classrooms "noticing and naming":

> Children becoming literate need to learn the significant features of text, how it relates to spoken language, how to recognize little tricks authors use to compel readers, when to use which sort of written language and so forth. However, no learner can afford to be dependent on the teacher for everything that needs to be noticed, so teachers have to teach children to look for possibilities. (2004, 17)

It's a fact that when my kids can't help themselves from noticing and pointing out characteristics of texts, teaching nonfiction writing becomes a whole lot more interesting and a whole lot easier.

Below are some examples of books we've read in nonfiction reading-for-writing time and ways we name what we notice. As the children talk about what they've noticed, I help them frame this noticing into a teaching point, or possibility for their own writing. I typically save the procedural or advice writing books as examples to use when we begin our procedural study after the nonfiction features study is completed. In both studies, we chart what we learn about nonfiction writing from these books, and the anchor chart hangs in the room for further reference throughout each study.

Books with Strong Visual Features

Reptiles: A Close-Up Look at Our Cold Blooded Cousins by Sue Malyan

"Nonfiction writers sometimes use boxes or bubbles to highlight facts or amazing information in their book." —Robby

Earthworms by Lola M. Schaefer (Heinemann Read and Learn Series; also in this series: *Jellyfish, Leeches, Newts,* and *Sea Anemones*)

"Nonfiction writers sometimes label the pictures in their book so the reader understands even more." —Margaux

Hottest, Coldest, Highest, Deepest by Steve Jenkins

"Nonfiction writers sometimes make comparisons between two things to help the reader understand the size of something." —Haley

Duckling by Lisa Magloff (DK Watch Me Grow Series; also in this series: *Ape, Bear, Frog, Kitten, Penguin, Puppy,* and *Turtle*)

"Nonfiction writers sometimes uses time lines or life cycles with pictures to show the growth of something over time." —Mark

Why Does Lightning Strike? by Terry Martin (DK Why? Series)

"Nonfiction writers sometimes begin each page with a question in the subtitle and then answer that question with the writing on the page." —Gabriel

Books That Represent a Specific Style or Craft of Writing

Atlantic by G. Brian Karas

"Sometimes writers of nonfiction put on the mask of the character and write 'I statements' through the book to hook the reader." —Gabriel

Are You a Butterfly? by Judy Allen and Tudor Humphries (Backyard Books series)

"Nonfiction writers sometimes start their book with a question and then answer that question through the pages." —Mark

It's a Frog's Life or *It's an Ant's Life* by Steve Parker

"Nonfiction writers sometimes make their book look like a real diary or journal with photos and notes taped inside along with the writing." —Haley

Earthworms by Lola M. Schaefer (Heinemann Read and Learn Series)

"Nonfiction writers sometimes write in a question and answer format, with subheadings and questions and information on the page answering that question." —Margaux

What Do You Do With a Tail Like This? and *What Do You Do When Something Wants to Eat You?* by Steve Jenkins and *Faces Only a Mother Could Love* by Jennifer Owings Dewey

"Writers of nonfiction work to capture their readers' attention by creating a catchy title." —Cecilia

Bat Loves the Night and *Ice Bear* by Nicola Davies

"Sometimes nonfiction writers combine a story with nonfiction information. Two kinds of text (fiction and nonfiction) are running at the top and bottom of the page." —Leo

Books That Represent the Procedural (How-To) Style of Writing

Super Snacks: Step by Step by Bobbie Kalman

Red Lace, Yellow Lace: Learn to Tie Your Shoes by Mike Casey

How to Be a Baby—By Me, The Big Sister by Sally Lloyd-Jones

How to Tell Time Klutz Publishers

Making Ice Cream, Making a Bug Habitat, Making a Weather Station by Natalie Lunis, and *Coin Magic* and *Make a Bird Feeder* by Cathy French (Benchmark Publishers How-To series)

Make Colors and *Make a Banana Treat* by Gill Budgell, and *Do the Lolly Trick* and *Make a Paper Hat* by Sarah Fleming

Try This by Monica Hughes and *How to Make a Bird Feeder* by Liyala Tuckfield (Rigby StarQuest series)

I Can Draw Animals, I Can Draw Machines, or others from the DK I Can Draw series

I want my students to become familiar with and use the features of nonfiction to support the reader's understanding.

As we read and notice different features writers use in nonfiction, the children and I make a chart with the name of the feature, what the feature is, why it's included in a text, and a picture example of the feature. *Nonfiction in Focus* by Janice V. Kristo and Rosemary A. Bamford was one key professional text that supported my understanding of how to help students become writers and readers of nonfiction, and their work helped me further scaffold my young writers into a better understanding of the features of nonfiction. As students read from the nonfiction section of our library every morning, they have the option of using a checklist to document the specific features they discover. On this checklist the students record the title of the book and page number where the feature was found so that they have a written reminder of the discovery and can share this new way the writer conveyed information. Figure 7.2 is a chart we developed in our class that became a key reference for the children as they were reading informational texts each morning and beginning to add some of these features to their writing.

In the classroom, I have an oversized chart of the text features students discover in their nonfiction genre reading each morning. As the children discover and name these features, I make a color copy of the feature from the book and paste it beside the definition so that children can also have a visual example of what the feature looks like in a real text.

Figures 7.3 and 7.4 show examples of text features from the published pieces of former students in first grade. They created these features to support the writing and help communicate nonfiction information to their readers.

So that children can envision what their text features might look like within an informational piece of writing, I intentionally create rough draft writing templates with text feature boxes added to the lined paper. A variety of paper choices and templates gives the children a support and an idea of what their writing might look like. These choices also provide a scaffold for children who have no sense of how to begin a piece or have a limited vision of the types of informational writing that are possible. I create a variety of paper templates to open the possibilities and choices in our nonfiction writing study. In our writing supply area, you will find papers designed to look like a blank page right out of a nonfiction text. Over the years I've also created templates for letters, menus, invitations, thank-you notes, brochures, and magazine or newspaper articles. The nonfiction genre is full of possibilities for study, and these are just a few of the kinds of writing you might explore with your students.

Fig. 7.2 Nonfiction Text Features

Name of Feature	What It Is	How It Supports the Reader's Understanding
Blurb	Brief description of the text	Captures the reader's interest or attention
Caption	Statement about a photo or illustration	Explains a photograph or an illustration
Cutaway	Picture where the outside is removed to show the inside parts	Gives the reader a view inside an object
Comparison	Photo or illustration relating two or more things based on similarities and differences	Compares or relates two or more things to one another
Diagram	A picture of an object and its parts	Identifies parts of something
Glossary	A list (alphabetized) of unusual words and definitions (usually at back of text)	Gives definitions of unfamiliar words
Graph	Representation of data	Shows information in a visual form (picture, line, pie graph)
Label	Describing word or phrase for a photo or illustration	Identifies an object or a place
Subheading	Title or description of a small part of text	Organizes the text clearly and gives more information about the text
Types of print (**boldface** and *italics*)	Words or phrases that are darker or slanted and different from the bulk of the text on a page	Helps the reader slow down and take note of important words or information

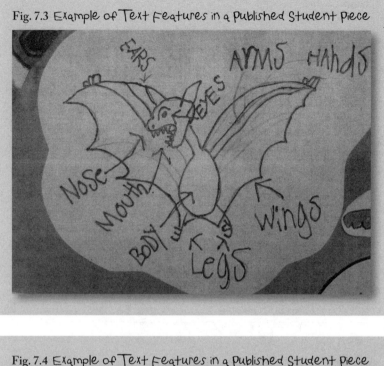

Fig. 7.3 Example of Text Features in a Published Student Piece

Fig. 7.4 Example of Text Features in a Published Student Piece

Our procedural writing study is a separate study from the one in which we focus on nonfiction features, but I provide the same kind of support, deliberately creating writing template paper that will give students a clear vision of the structure and contents of this type of nonfiction writing. During our procedural writing study in past years, students have used (1) an introduction page, to introduce their reader to the topic in the book; (2) a materials list page, with spaces for both listing and illustrating the tools and materials necessary for carrying out the how-to project; (3) a step-by-step template page with separate lines for writing each step alongside a box for the illustration of that step; (4) an about the author template page, used in many of our publications to tell the reader about the author and the reason for writing the piece. You can see how Wesley used the step-by-step templates to write "How to Draw a Person Good!" shown in Figure 7.5.

I want my students to write dash facts from their reading, talking, and research so that the information is specific and clear, but isn't copied directly from the text.

Over the years I've found that my primary students are naturally

Fig. 7.5 "How to Draw a Person Good!": Wesley's How-To Piece

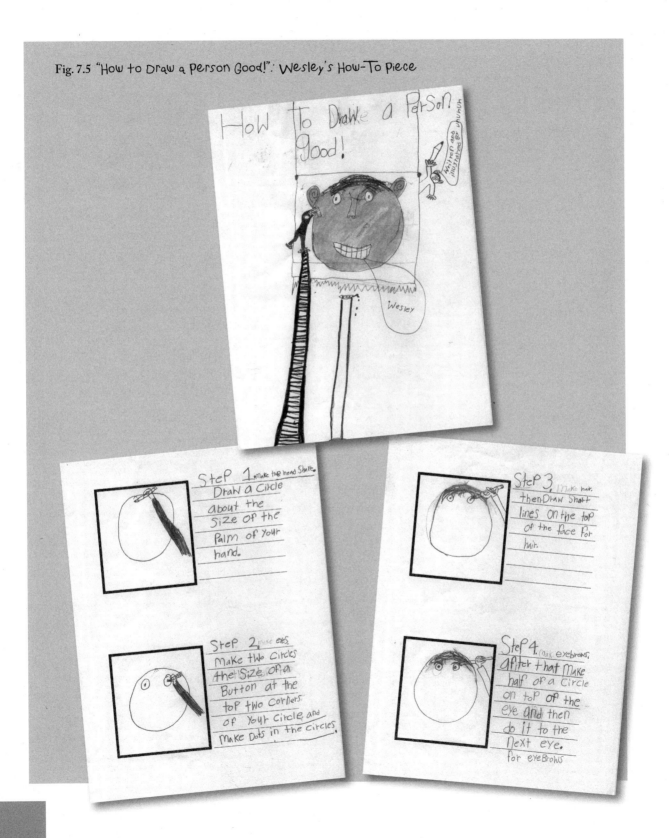

Fig. 7.5 (continued) "How to Draw a Person Good!": Wesley's How-To Piece

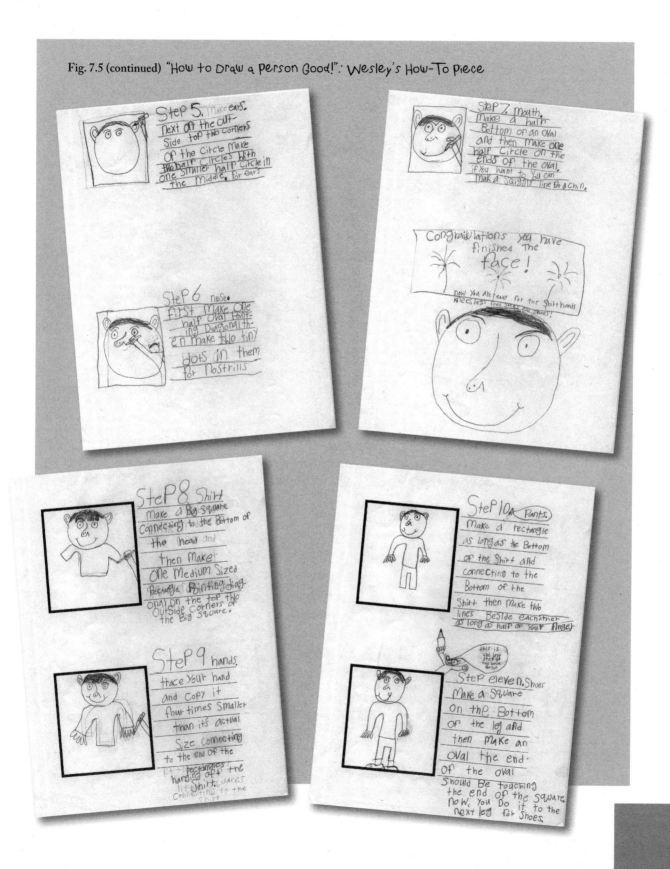

interested in *lots* of nonfiction topics and want to write about those topics of interest, but they don't necessarily have the background knowledge about the topic to produce a content-filled, engaging text.

Can't you just picture this? Sally meets me at the table for a conference and quickly states, "I'm writing a book about tigers!" and I have the young tiger lover staring me straight in the face with a stack of blank paper and a black and an orange crayon in each fist. When "So tell me, Sally, what are you going to teach your reader about tigers?" is quickly answered with, "I don't really know that much about tigers, but I *really like* them!" we know it's time to teach the child about reading (or looking at pictures, photographs, and features in a text) and notetaking to build background knowledge. One of the best ways I've found to help young students take notes without copying directly from the text is by teaching them to write dash facts.

I first learned of the term *dash fact* from Ralph Fletcher and JoAnn Portalupi, and their son Joseph's first-grade teacher, Jane Winsor. I found that this terminology helped students understand the concept of notetaking, that it's not giving the reader everything, but simply a "dash" of important information. Like a dash of salt added to a recipe—that dash of salt is a key ingredient in making the dish tasty and complete, but if the entire salt shaker were added, the dish would be ruined. When writing dash facts, students understand that what they've given the reader is a dash of information—not the whole paragraph or page, just the dash that's important to make the writing interesting, complete, informative, and "tasty" for the reader. One way I've encouraged students to write these dash facts is to read short segments of text and then close their books. They then think about what they've just read and write a dash of important information that they've learned. Jonathan's dash facts on lions are shown in Figure 7.6.

This work ensures that students build their background knowledge about a subject and write about that subject in ways that are understandable and developmentally appropriate. When our primary writers' research sounds like it came straight from an encyclopedia, that's our clue to give students

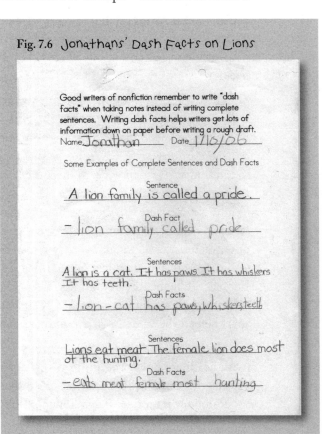

Fig. 7.6 Jonathans' Dash Facts on Lions

Good writers of nonfiction remember to write "dash facts" when taking notes instead of writing complete sentences. Writing dash facts helps writers get lots of information down on paper before writing a rough draft.

Name Jonathan   Date 1/16/06

Some Examples of Complete Sentences and Dash Facts

Sentence
A lion family is called a pride.

Dash Fact
- lion family called pride

Sentences
A lion is a cat. It has paws. It has whiskers. It has teeth.

Dash Facts
- lion - cat has paws, whiskers, teeth

Sentences
Lions eat meat. The female lion does most of the hunting.

Dash Facts
- eats meat female most hunting

strategies for learning new information and writing about that information in ways that make sense. Dash facts are a great way to begin this process with your young writers.

I want my students to organize factual information into subheadings, subcategories, or steps.

Once students have learned to take notes (or even if they've moved to writing a complete rough draft), primary students tend to ignore organization of the information they've written about their topic. Many times they write and write and write with no attention to how that information will be conveyed to the reader. This is when focus lessons or conferences around rereading, organizing, and categorizing notes and facts are helpful. Appendix D includes an example of a support sheet for organization.

In the past, I've had my students reread notes they've taken and actually cut those notes apart into separate facts. Then, they organize the facts according to common themes. For example, if a child has written about an animal, any fact connected to where the animal lives might go under a subheading titled Habitat. Notes about what the animal eats might go under the subheading Food. This sounds simple, but naming subheadings and organizing notes is a skill that requires lots of modeling and practice for young writers. The physical act of cutting the notes and facts apart and rearranging them helps students think about commonalities among the facts and helps them organize their pieces for readers. It also helps students see where information is missing or details are limited and the text needs beefing up.

Also, when working on text organization, I have students think about a statement in their nonfiction writing and then imagine that piece of information under a subheading in the table of contents. Where might it fit? For example, if a student has written *Penguins have flippers and webbed feet*, he or she might determine that this information would be found under "Parts of a Penguin's Body" in the table of contents. Sometimes, before the students cut the facts into separate pieces of paper, they label each fact with an abbreviation, or note about where this fact might fit in the text. For example, some of my students labeled facts *a.c.*, which stood for attributes and characteristics—or facts that describe the features or characteristics of an animal they researched. Sometimes I'd find *d.y.k.b.* alongside some of the notes the children had taken. I quickly learned that this stood for "Did You Know...? Bubble"—like the title of our informational posters, but in this case a bit of information the students thought should stand out as an amazing fact. Labeling notes before cutting them apart helped the students in their text organization.

With a whole class or in small groups, I use Big Books or texts on the overhead projector (with headings and subheadings covered) and have discussions about what these headings or categories might be, based on the information on the page. This reading and talking about organization then helps students when they get ready to organize their own writing.

Organization in writing is a skill students will work to improve for years to come, and it's important for young writers to have experience reading and talking about how texts are organized before they are expected to try organizing and categorizing their own writing.

Because the skill of organization is a sophisticated one for young writers, and because young children are naturally "drawn" to drawing and illustrating before putting lots of text on a page, I first pursued the nonfiction features focus study with my students. This study allowed students to study, discover, illustrate, and use nonfiction features like labels, captions, diagrams, close-ups, and cutaways while at the same time teaching their readers without having to rely heavily on text and organization. These features the students were studying and would use to teach readers would eventually support and extend further writing on the topic. Once students were able to publish their own nonfiction features poster—the Did You Know… ? Bubble—I was then able to support the students in pursuing longer nonfiction texts with more writing and features that supported that writing.

When we are learning to write how-to pieces, the best way I've found to teach my students to appropriately organize their writing is to have the students act out or actually do what they are teaching their readers to do—whether it's how to draw a flower, how to tie a shoe, or how to take care of a baby sister, it's important for young children to actually follow the steps that they are writing in these how-to pieces. It's also helpful for me to put myself in the position of learner or "direction follower" when my writers share their how-to pieces. That way the class can watch me follow a student's directions exactly (and participate in helping their classmate clarify directions when I'm not clear on what to do).

For example, one day at the end of writing workshop, Rylee eagerly shares her piece, "How to Draw a Ladybug." She says to the class, "First draw a circle," and since I'm pretending to be the direction follower as Rylee reads her piece, I quickly draw a giant circle at the top of my blank piece of chart paper. Squeals from the class of "Miss Corgill! That's too big! Ladybugs don't look like that!" "Ladybugs don't fly as high as the sun and you drew it up high in the sky!" Rylee assures me that it's "all wrong," and my first attempt at her direction causes a quick revision of the first step. "Okay, Miss Corgill. First, draw a circle about the size of a penny in the center of the page." And I revise my illustration.

As I follow each step, the children are eager to help Rylee make her writing more specific, clear, and organized by using directional words (*bottom right*) and comparisons to give an estimate of size (about the size of a penny, oval and about the size of an egg, four times smaller than your hand). They also insist that steps need words like *first, next, then,* and *finally* to give the reader a clearer sense of the order in which the steps are followed. The class is also eager to let Rylee know when she's left out a critical step for her readers. "So what color is this ladybug?! You didn't tell us what color markers we would need to color the body!" "Do you draw the leaf that the ladybug will sit on before you draw the body of the ladybug?" Questions such as these arise almost daily in our writing share times during the procedural study, and these questions are perfect opportunities for teaching about organization and clarity within this genre.

I want my students to write with "voice and personality."

Earthworms eat dead plants. They eat leaves, roots, stems, and seeds. Earthworms eat dirt. They eat bugs. All true facts about earthworms, right? And all *very* dry and boring writing! Young nonfiction writers are experts at writing pages and pages of fact-filled *but* extremely dry, lifeless, and boring writing. I have found this particularly true when students are writing how-to or procedural texts. As I sat through numerous just-put-me-out-of-my-misery nonfiction writing share times and conferences, I began to realize the importance of teaching young writers how to add voice and personality to their pieces. Some of the ways I've helped students add life to their writing is to study and think about these possible crafting techniques:

- Writing from a different perspective (or writing through a mask, as my students and I like to call it)

- Having conversations with the reader and making comments to the reader throughout the text

- Embedding questions to the reader throughout the text

- Stating opinions and reacting to the facts written

During one of our how-to studies, Amanda Cort, a former MNS second grader, had lots of friends in class and decided to teach her readers how to make and keep good friends. She recognized that sometimes everyone deals with breakups in friendships. Figure 7.7 shows her advice for surviving those traumatic times with friends. Amanda's voice also shines through as she gives her readers suggestions for what to do when you're hanging out with a potential best friend. It's the student's voice in a piece that many times reflects his or her opinions about a topic. When voice and personality are added to a once dry and lifeless piece, students then begin to recognize the difference between true facts and personal opinion. It's these additions of opinions, questions, reactions, and conversations from the child that give life to the facts in the piece.

I want my students to publish and reflect on nonfiction writing about a specific topic.

My students have published their work in a variety of ways over the years, and a few of these publishing possibilities are found in Chapter 9, with specific tips and techniques for producing gorgeous, fact-filled pieces of writing and visual displays. In Figures 7.8 and 7.9 you'll find examples of student reflections on their work as nonfiction writers. See Appendix D for a blank writing journey reflection sheet for a nonfiction features study.

Fig. 7.7 "Friends Forever": Amanda's How-To piece

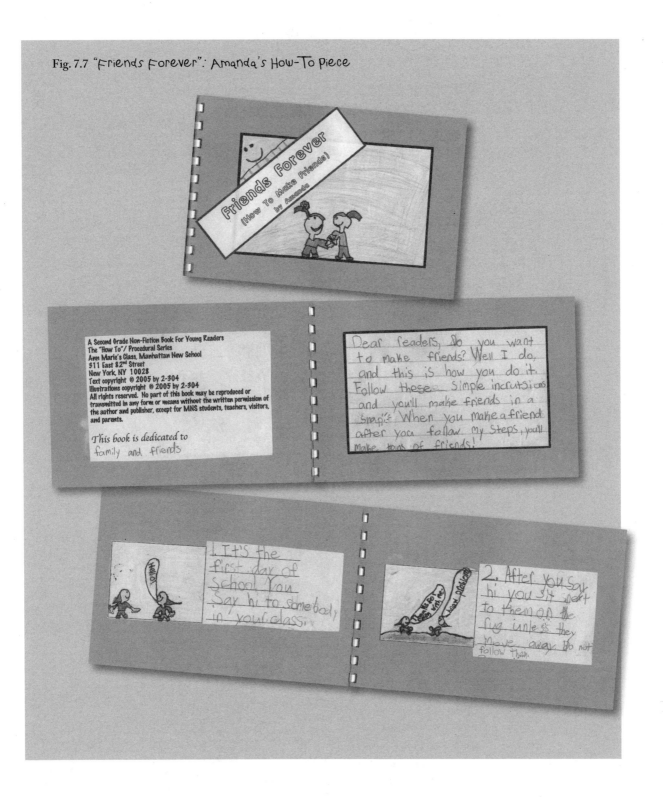

Fig. 7.7 (continued) "Friends Forever": Amanda's How-To piece

3. You hug them xsept ask them to make sure if they don't like to be touched.

4. You tell them a joke like "knok knok." Who's there? Boo? Boo who? Why are you cring?

5. Hug them even more. Only if they say you can hug them.

6. You made a friend!

Suggested Activities For You And Your New Friends
1. Go to the movies.
2. Tell them they can come over.
3. Take them to a Bradway Play.
4. Go to a Festrant with them.
5. Ask them if they want to get their nails done with you.

Tips For Handling a New Friend Breakup
1. Try to be as nice as you can. If that doesn't work
2. Try to talk to them. If that doesn't work
3. Tell another friend.
4. Make new friends.
5. The other friend will get board and she will want to be your friend again or you'll have more friends.

About The Author
Amanda Cort is seven years old. She is in Secand grade. She doesn't have any brothers or sisters or a dog, but she is going to get one soon. She has many friends right now and this book is about her strategies to make more friends.

Fig. 7.8 Anthea's Reflection from the NonFiction Features Study

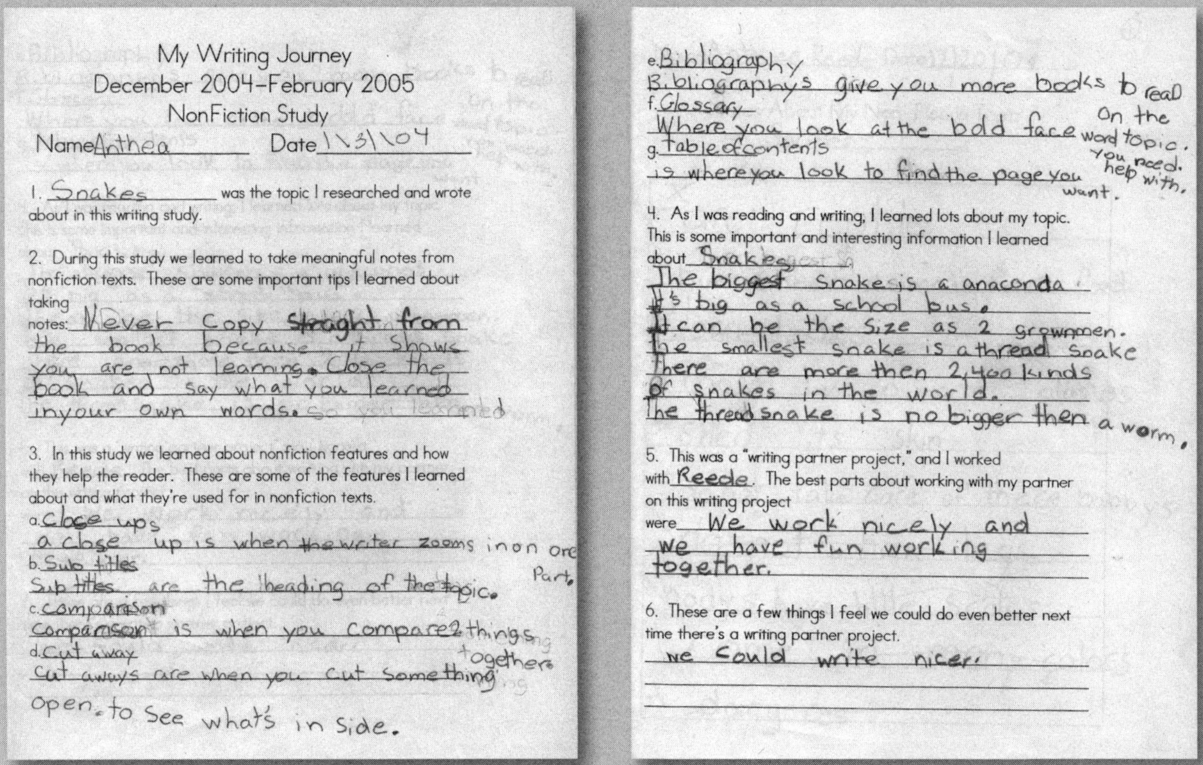

My Writing Journey
December 2004–February 2005
NonFiction Study
Name Anthea   Date 1\31\04

1. Snakes   was the topic I researched and wrote about in this writing study.

2. During this study we learned to take meaningful notes from nonfiction texts. These are some important tips I learned about taking notes: Never copy straight from the book because it shows you are not learning. Close the book and say what you learned in your own words.

3. In this study we learned about nonfiction features and how they help the reader. These are some of the features I learned about and what they're used for in nonfiction texts.
a. Close ups
   a close up is when the writer zooms in on one part.
b. Sub titles
   Sub titles are the heading of the topic.
c. Comparison
   Comparison is when you compare 2 things together.
d. Cut away
   cut aways are when you cut something open to see what's inside.

e. Bibliography
   Bibliographys give you more books to read on the topic.
f. Glossary
   Where you look at the bold face word you need help with.
g. table of contents
   is where you look to find the page you want.

4. As I was reading and writing, I learned lots about my topic. This is some important and interesting information I learned about Snakes.
The biggest snake is a anaconda.
It's big as a school bus.
It can be the size as 2 growmen.
The smallest snake is a thread snake
there are more then 2,400 kinds of snakes in the world.
The thread snake is no bigger then a worm.

5. This was a "writing partner project," and I worked with Reede. The best parts about working with my partner on this writing project were We work nicely and we have fun working together.

6. These are a few things I feel we could do even better next time there's a writing partner project.
We could write nicer.

But most of all, I want my students to be forever curious.

I want to show children through our work as writers that the world is a glorious, amazing, and forever changing place. It is my hope that our work in writing and reading will only enhance and support the students' understanding that it is our job (and our freedom) to continue to ask questions, to wonder, to debate, to learn facts, to give opinions, and to remain forever curious.

Writing is the way for young children to bring their world to life and continue to make sense of it. School should be the place that lights the fire of curiosity in our students and gives them opportunities to make sense of this wonderful world we live in. I sincerely believe that giving six-, seven-, and eight-year-olds daily opportunities both inside and outside school to write about their interests, their passions, their curiosities, and their expertise is the beginning of creating citizens who will lead our world and be passionate about our growth, our progress, and our future.

Figure 7.10 offers suggestions for teaching points during a conferences in a nonfiction unit of study.

Fig. 7.9 Noah's Reflection from the Procedural (How-To) Study

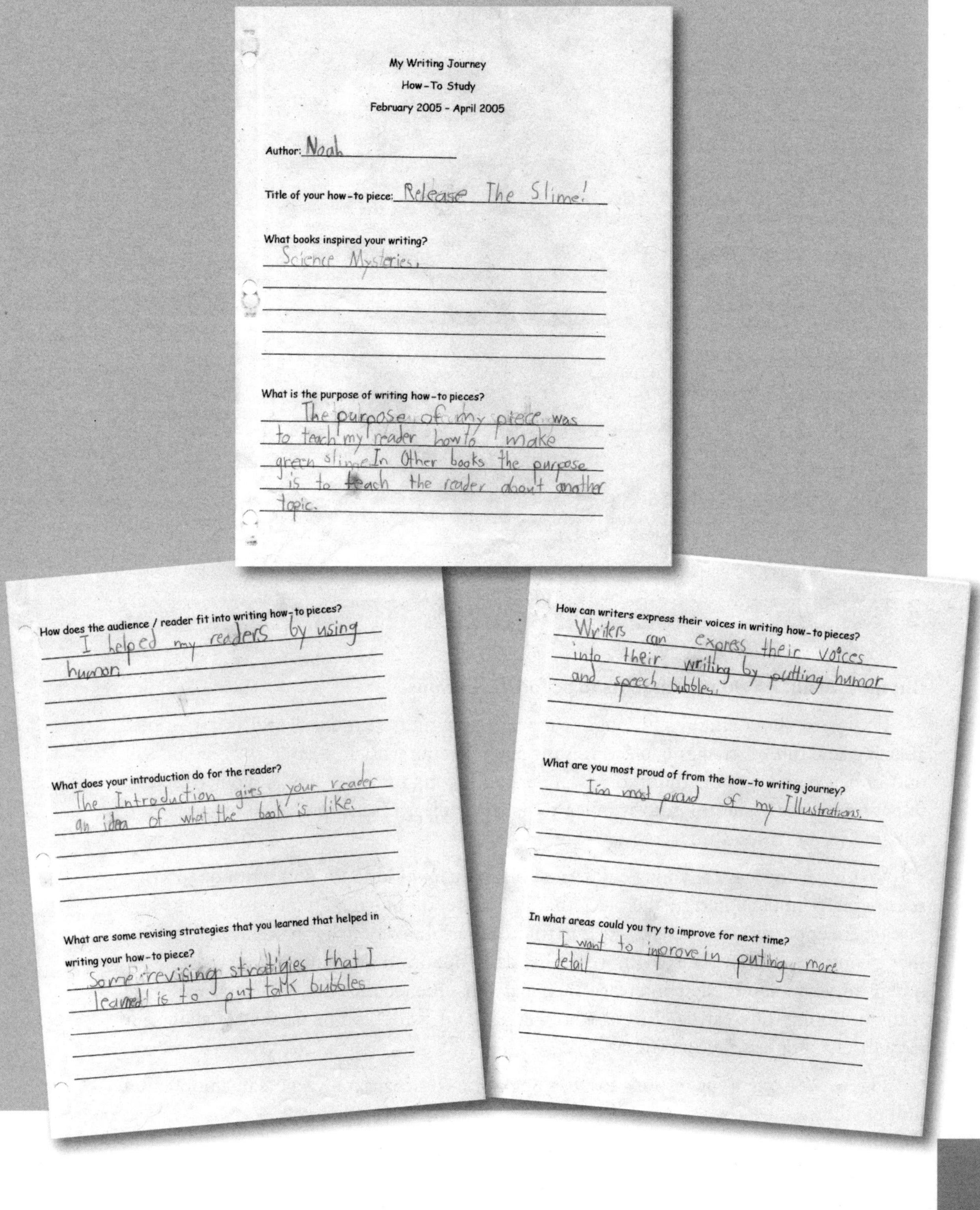

My Writing Journey

How-To Study

February 2005 – April 2005

Author: Noah

Title of your how-to piece: Release The Slime!

What books inspired your writing?
Science Mysteries.

What is the purpose of writing how-to pieces?
The purpose of my piece was to teach my reader how to make green slime. In Other books the purpose is to teach the reader about another topic.

How does the audience / reader fit into writing how-to pieces?
I helped my readers by using humor.

What does your introduction do for the reader?
The Introduction gives your reader an idea of what the book is like.

What are some revising strategies that you learned that helped in writing your how-to piece?
Some revising stratigies that I learned is to put talk bubbles.

How can writers express their voices in writing how-to pieces?
Writers can express their voices into their writing by putting humor and speech bubbles.

What are you most proud of from the how-to writing journey?
I'm most proud of my Illustrations.

In what areas could you try to improve for next time?
I want to improve in putting more detail.

Fig. 7.10 Possible Teaching Points for Primary Writers Pursuing a Nonfiction Unit of Study

Situation	Teaching Point
If the writer comes to a conference with little to no background knowledge or information about their topic	Growing writers of nonfiction sometimes have to read first before they write to build background knowledge about a subject.
If the writer comes to the conference with lots of information about his or her topic all written on one or two pages	Growing writers of nonfiction sometimes use subheadings to get the reader ready for what they will learn on a page of writing.
If the writer comes to the conference with information copied directly from the text they are reading.	Growing writers of nonfiction work to write the information they read in their own words. 1. Read. 2. Close the book. 3. Think. 4. Write what you know.
If the writer comes to the conference with only writing and little to no visual information	Growing writers of nonfiction sometimes teach their readers using diagrams (labeling parts of an illustration to give the reader more info). Growing writers of nonfiction sometimes add cutaways to their writing so the reader can see the inside of something. Growing writers of nonfiction sometimes add illustrations with labels to their writing to give the reader more visual information.
If the young writer comes to the conference with a significant amount of text that is organized and rich in content but has no access features to help the reader	Growing writers of nonfiction sometimes add a table of contents or an index to their writing to help the reader locate information in the book.
If the writer is struggling with notetaking and comes to the conference with notes written in complete sentences	When growing writers of nonfiction take notes, they write dash facts, including a dash of important information minus the unnecessary words like *a, and,* and *the.*
If the writer comes to the conference and wants to add a glossary or index to his or her piece of writing	Growing writers of nonfiction use boldfaced words to make the reader stop and think, "This word is important for me to know!"

Chapter 8
Picture This
Teaching and Learning About Picture Books with Primary Writers

Picture Books: Unit of Study Curriculum Map

Key Provisions (what students must have)	Big Ideas (what students should understand)	Essential Skills and Concepts (what students should be able to do)	Possible Text Supports (what students might use to support their work)	Assessment (what students will complete as documentation of growth)
• Topic choice • Daily writing time • Opportunities for writers to read the kinds of books they want to write • Demonstration, practice, teaching, and celebration during workshop period • Opportunities for writers to write a variety of genres • A purpose for writing and an audience • Support from the other authors and teachers in the classroom (students, teachers, books by published authors) • Tools necessary for writers to write and publish the kinds of pieces they envision • Time for writers to think, talk, write, and share every day	• Picture books can have a variety of structures and layouts. • A variety of media and illustrating techniques can be used to support the writing in the text and create meaning. • Meaning can be made from choices in size, color, and placement of words in a picture book. • Picture books can be written from different perspectives. • Picture books can be written in one specific genre or there may be genre overlap in one book. • The writing on each page of a picture book is connected to make meaning from beginning to end. • Picture books are written for different purposes and audiences.	• Choose a topic appropriate for the audience • Write rough drafts and reread those drafts for editing and revising • Illustrate to support the words in the text • Choose a title that catches the reader's attention and supports the writing • Use different sizes and colors in illustrations and words to convey meaning or emotion • Use appropriate punctuation to convey meaning or emotion • Write with voice and personality, using interesting vocabulary, sound effects, or dialogue • Publish a piece/story with a clear and connected beginning, middle, and end • Write an "about the author" for the piece	• *Grandpa's Soup* by Eiko Kadono • *My Brother* by Anthony Browne • *It's Going to Be Perfect* by Nancy Carlson • *The Story of Grump and Pout!* by Jamie McEwan • *How to Be a Baby—By Me, the Big Sister* by Sally Lloyd-Jones and Sue Heap • *My Big Sister* by Valorie Fisher • *My Map Book* by Sara Fanelli • *Good Night, Pillow Fight* by Sally Cook • *Get Red* by Tony Porto • *Being Friends* by Karen Beaumont • *Do You Know What I'll Do?* by Charlotte Zolotow • *What Makes Me Happy?* by Catherine and Laurence Anholt • *Courage* by Bernard Waber • *Serendipity* by Tobi Tobias • *The Incredible Book Eating Boy* by Oliver Jeffers • *Scaredy Squirrel* by Mélanie Watt	• What We Know About Picture Book Writing and Illustrating charts • Student work samples from beginning, middle, and end of study • Videotapes of writing share and conferences during the study • Rough and final draft work • Writing journey reflection • Published picture book

> *I wanted a perfect ending… Now I've learned, the hard way, that some poems*
> *don't rhyme, and some stories don't have a clear beginning, middle, and end…*
> *Life is about not knowing, having to change, taking the moment and making*
> *the best of it, without knowing what's going to happen next. Delicious ambiguity.*
>
> —Gilda Radner

When I taught in Westchester County, New York, our school was severely damaged by a spring nor'easter. Floodwaters destroyed the first floor of the building, leaving the office, gym, auditorium, cafeteria, and every kindergarten class in utter destruction. Many of the teachers lost everything. Years and years of teaching and planning. Gone. Everything from books to blocks were submerged in five feet of water. Pet turtles were found swimming among the Legos, and children's artwork and writing dissolved right before the eyes of the rescue team. What do you do in times like these? You rise above the floodwaters. That's just what my amazing colleagues did, and this was our opportunity to take each moment and make the best of it. It was time to do what really matters—to teach our students about life and about how to re-create happy endings.

A Reason for Writing

My students and I lived in one of the lucky second-floor classrooms spared from the floodwaters. We still had all our books, all our materials, all our work, and it was heartbreaking to watch helplessly as friends sifted through the destruction in their classrooms. What could we do to help? To be honest, before the flood happened, this last writing study of the year had me stumped. I knew I wanted to take the time to revisit all we had learned about writing since September, but I wasn't quite sure how to present this study to the class. The kids had learned lots about writing, believed they were authors, and continued to do all the things that writers do each day at school.

And now a purpose for the study was staring me straight in the face. If there had ever been a time to make the work we do count in the world outside our classroom, it was now. Our last writing study of the year would be to use what we'd learned over the past nine months about quality writing and do something important with that knowledge. We would write books to read to our friends, the kindergarten teachers and students, who now shared spaces in the computer lab down the hall and in the science and music rooms on the third floor and were working so hard to re-create new classroom libraries and homes.

Everything our class had learned this year about audience and purpose and craft and engagement and writing for your readers would truly come to life. This writing, these books the children would author and then read aloud, would be a way to bring happiness to kindergarten children whose classroom libraries were destroyed by the floodwaters. There's not much else to say except, What better reason than this to write?

How to Begin

We had the *why*, the reason for our study, and now it was time for me to plan the *how*. Because my kids wanted to write books to read to the kindergarten students, I thought the best way to pursue this work would be to study and look specifically at our favorite picture books and how those books were written. Remember, these are first-grade students writing to their kindergarten peers, so I had to work especially hard to make this picture book study one in which my six- and seven-year-olds could feel successful and accomplished.

I typically envision a strong and thorough picture book study being pursued in older grades because there is so much to learn and discover about this genre. There are so many great books out there, so many authors, so many styles, and so many award winners. I do confess that it's a bit scary to pursue something so big with writers who are so little. It's very easy to fall into a prestudy panic attack when I also envision the never-ending, going-nowhere-fast, multi-topic, multi-chapter, dialogue-dominant craziness that first graders typically write when left to their own wits and experience. But thinking back to the progress we had made since the first study of the year and remembering one of my favorite quotes from *Alice in Wonderland*, I'm "believing this impossible thing before breakfast" in the dark at my computer. It's that belief and the possibilities to support my students in making a difference in their school that makes this study worth pursuing. I believe that as a class we can revisit what we've learned about quality writing, study those texts we've read and reread (now as writers), and then write well-crafted, perfectly appropriate first-grade picture books with smart endings, focused topics, connected contents, and balanced dialogue. Come with me now and let's take a look at some of the highlights and important points in a primary picture book study.

Tools

Let's first talk about the tools the students and I will need to work through this study.

Paper Choices

I created paper choices in this study that would scaffold students in producing both text and illustrations in a clear and organized way. (See the picture book paper choice in Appendix E.)

Rough Draft Folders

These folders have housed all the writing and illustrating the children have done since September, and they'll use these folders again for their final study of the year. Each day as they work on part of their piece, I will ask that they date their pages so that I can see the progression of the work over the course of the weeks. I ask that the children throw nothing away because every piece they produce in some way shows the journey toward their goal. The steps in the journey are just as important as the destination.

Illustrating Utensils/Mediums

Because we will be studying the variety of ways illustrators work and create pictures to support the writing of picture book authors, I will provide multiple materials and art supplies for use in this study. Children will be able to use crayons, colored pencils, oil pastels, colored paper, watercolors, tempera paints, collage papers, tissue paper, and digital camera photos. As we study possible ways to illustrate, I will introduce the medium in the workshop focus lesson or work time during the day.

Picture Books to Guide the Study

Please refer to the lists and book suggestions throughout this chapter for use in focus lessons and morning genre reading time.

Audience and Topic Selection

Naturally, when I proposed this picture book idea, my students were thrilled to have the opportunity to write for their friends and were already proudly imagining how their books would look when published and sitting on the shelves of the kindergarten classrooms.

Much of what we would do in this unit would be a review or a culmination of all that we had studied in previous units throughout the year along with new work focusing specifically on the genre of picture books. To begin the study I asked the children to think about their interests as kindergarten children and to think back to the studies they pursued last year. In this first lesson I reminded the children that when writers work on a new piece, they think about the audience they are writing to and for. I charted what the children remembered about their kindergarten experience, and we quickly realized that much of what the students remembered as important topics, experiences, and passions from kindergarten were still very important to them as first graders. That's what's great about writing for someone who's practically your own age—they have interests similar to your own!

Now that we had information about our audience, our readers, we could begin the process of topic selection. My students studied the lists of topics we charted and thought about their interests, passions, and background knowledge about these subjects. Like many students at this age, Nan loved *everything* about kindergarten, so she decided to write about all the places she loved in that first year of school. Mark quickly decided to engage in a superhero story about a "guy who fights bad weather and can get rid of floods." And we wonder where that idea came from? Learning the ABCs was a milestone for Robby in his first year of school, so he decided to teach his kindergarten friends the letters with a food alphabet book.

Leo began to write about computers, Haley about two sisters who loved cats and bought a curious cat from the pet store. Griffin began to create a "super skateboarder" piece showing how the novice becomes the "best skateboarder in the world." From baseball and soccer and basketball to rainbows and rain forests and friendships, the children were well on their way to beginning their last masterpiece of the year.

Student Discoveries

Each morning the children started the day with picture book reading and then genre share at our morning meeting. Before the study began, I carefully selected picture books that I thought would encourage conversation and be clear in presenting ideas about topic, craft, and structure to the children. I looked for books with the following characteristics:

- Predictable patterns
- Repetitive language
- A variety of mediums in the illustrations—photographs, watercolor, paper collage, acrylic, mosaic, and simple crayon or colored pencil illustrations
- Topics suitable for primary-grade writers
- Different perspectives
- An additional story in the illustrations
- Familiarity—books that we had previously read in reading workshop and could now explore through the eyes of writers

On day one of our study we began a chart titled What We're Noticing About the Writing and Illustrating in Picture Books, and this chart guided our share and focus lessons for the next several weeks. Each day as the children shared their discoveries, I charted the information and included their names and the books in which they discovered the technique, craft, or structure so that we could refer to these books in focus lessons, conferences, and when writing our own pieces. (See Figure 8.1.)

Some of the "noticings" of the children during our morning genre-reading time follow. You'll find their names with their discoveries. For the children, seeing their names in print on a chart that hangs prominently in the room created a greater investment and ownership in the work they were doing as authors and illustrators and "writing investigators."

- Illustrations/color of pictures helps to show feelings (Devin and Gabriela) from *Grandpa's Soup*

- Use a repeating word or line (Andrew and Mark) from *My Brother* and *It's Going to Be Perfect*

- Size of words shows feeling WAIT!!, STOP!! (Leo) from *The Story of Grump and Pout!*

- Author puts on a mask and pretends to be the character (Gabriel, Griffin, and Jamie) from *How to Be a Baby—By Me, the Big Sister* and *My Big Sister*

- There's a changing point (Grace) from *It's Going to Be Perfect*

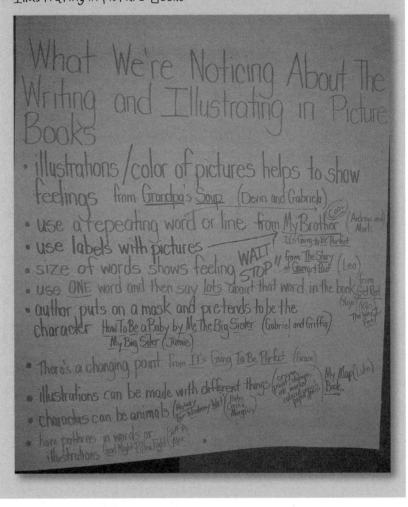

Fig. 8.1 Chart of Discoveries About the Writing and Illustrating in Picture Books

- Illustrations can be made with different things (crayons, paint, stamps, ink, marker, colored pencil, paper, pencil) (Luke) from *My Map Book*

- Characters can be animals (Haley, Cecilia, and Margaux) from *Hooway for Wodney Wat*

- Have patterns in words or illustrations (Jeff and Alex) from *Good Night, Pillow Fight*

- Uses *one* word and then says *lots* about that word in the book (Yuya and Kiki) from *Get Red* and *The Way I Feel*

My job as a primary writing teacher is to help children take ownership for their learning and to recognize that our success stems from what they bring to each class and each workshop. It's my job to help them see that their voices, their reading, their writing, and their discoveries guide my teaching. My job is to be the person to set them up for success. That's why I start each day with reading and sharing the discoveries of the children. I then use these discoveries to focus my teaching objectives and to know how to carry those objectives out in whole-class, small-group, and conference lessons.

Objectives

Let's first talk about meaning behind the objectives, and then look at how these objectives are carried out in the teaching times during the day.

I want students to learn about picture book structures, crafting techniques, and illustrating possibilities in this study. I think of these three objectives as an architect and interior designer would think of building and designing a house.

My first objective is to help students understand that books have a structure that holds the writing in place and supports a reader's understanding of the text.

Structures

When I speak of structure, I think of the frame of a house. The house frame provides a support for all the work that will be done around and inside the house. It gives the builders a place to start when they're ready to hang Sheetrock, lay brick, or hammer a roof. The structure of a picture book gives writers a place to start when they're ready to develop a topic, craft text, or sketch and color illustrations. How do I talk with primary writers about structure? In this particular study with these students, we focused on five very simple and recognizable structures.

- Opposites
- Question and Answer
- Repeating line with supporting details
- Lists
- Beginning/Changing Point/Ending

Opposites

This year my children named the opposite structure the "good/bad, happy/sad" structure to help them remember that the pages alternate with opposite feelings, beliefs, actions, ideas. Some picture books that help students see this structure and begin to envision their own structures are

Being Friends by Karen Beaumont

What's Up, What's Down by Lola M. Schaefer

Country Kid, City Kid by Julie Cummins

Question and Answer

Question and answer books are set up or structured with a main question first and then the answer to that question on the following pages. There may be one big question and the rest of the book is the answer to that question, or there may be multiple questions with the answers following each of the questions. Some picture books that support this idea and help students see the question and answer structure are

Do You Know What I'll Do? by Charlotte Zolotow

Who Is the World For? by Tom Pow

Have You Ever Done That? by Julie Larios

What Makes Me Happy? by Catherine and Laurence Anholt

Repeating Line with Supporting Detail

Primary students are quickly able to see repeating lines or words throughout the text, so it's easy to teach this structure to students as a possibility for their own writing. Some texts with repeating lines or phrases with supporting details are:

My Brother by Anthony Browne

It's Going to Be Perfect by Nancy Carlson

Lists

Using the list structure as a possibility is a great way to encourage those less prolific, hesitant writers in your classroom. These children see that authors don't always have to have word-heavy texts and can convey meaning with very few words written in list form. Alphabet books, number books, and "definition" books are just a few examples of this kind of structure. Some texts written in list form that we've read and studied are

Courage by Bernard Waber

Serendipity by Tobi Tobias

Get Red by Tony Porto

Fed Up by Rex Barron

The Way I Feel by Janan Cain

Beginning/Changing Point/Ending

The last structure is easy for primary students to identify but tends to be the most difficult to achieve in their own writing. This is the basic structure of all fiction books we read, and this is the one that typically makes teachers of young children think, "What do I do with this never-ending, going-nowhere, multi-chapter, multi-topic, dialogue-dominant nonsense?" I work to guide my most proficient writers with this structure while also steering less sophisticated writers in other structural directions. Not because I don't believe in their ideas, but because I want to teach the writers to pursue structures that they can developmentally handle and communicate with effectively. The children all know at this point in the year that our main goal is to help our readers understand and enjoy the writing we produce, and it's important for me to guide students in directions that will engage and support them (as well as their readers) in making sense of text. Some of my most recent picture book favorites that support this "beginning/changing point/ending" structure are

The Incredible Book Eating Boy by Oliver Jeffers

Scaredy Squirrel by Mélanie Watt

Scaredy Squirrel Makes a Friend Mélanie Watt

Once the structure, or the "frame," of a book is in place, the writer can then play with the design of the piece, using interesting language, punctuation, font sizes, sentence placement, and detailed illustrations.

Crafting Techniques

Not only do I want my primary writers to learn about how to structure a piece of writing, but I also want my students to go away with crafting techniques in their writing repertoires. What do I consider craft from a primary writing stance? I call my definition of *craft* the "Fletcher-Portalupi-Ray-Routman-Harwayne-Graves-Laminack-Calkins definition." My understanding of what it means to craft a piece of writing is a collage of thinking from my friends, mentors, and those brilliant writing educators whom I've never met. I believe that the evidence of craft in a piece of writing is a sign that the young author has learned to be intentional with word choice, spacing, punctuation, sound, and detail. Craft is about making those intentional choices for the purpose of creating writing that's meaningful and enjoyable for the reader.

When I speak of teaching children crafting techniques found in picture books, I think of this teaching like the interior designer would in designing spaces for living. The interior designer works so that the inhabitants stand back and say, "Wow, there's something special about this place." I imagine the owners taking a walk through their new house to admire the claw-foot bathtub, the pine plank living-room floors, the arched doorway to the kitchen, the farmhouse sink, and the stained-glass window overlooking the garden. Those are the special touches that make the homeowners stand back and take notice. Those are the special touches that are unique to the house itself and make it original. Those are the details that make the owners look forward to coming home again and again.

I believe that young writers can do work that's similar to the expert interior designer. I believe that children can learn crafting techniques that will cause their readers to stand back and take notice, to say, "Wow, there's something special about this piece." I believe that children can learn to use punctuation, sentence structure, and language in ways that bring their writing to life and engage readers. And because of that belief, my students and I will spend a large portion of this picture book study reading about, naming, and using specific crafting techniques in lessons and workshop time. We do this so that our readers will look forward to reading and coming back to these books again and again.

These were some specific crafting techniques we studied in this unit:

- Repeating words or phrases
- Font sizes and italics
- Sound effects
- Word and letter placement
- Talk bubbles/thinking bubbles
- Leads and endings
- Mask writing
- 20/20 words

Illustrating Possibilities

I also think of an interior designer choosing paint colors to match curtains and furniture, creating color schemes to evoke a sense of calm or a look of subtle softness. Illustrators of picture books work in ways similar to the architect and the interior designer. The illustrations in a picture book are so deeply connected to the writing and oftentimes enhance the work far greater than we realize. In this study, I devote at least half of the time to studying picture book illustrations with my students. We also create a chart titled What We're Noticing About Picture Book Illustrations to guide our work in the writing and illustrating workshop.

Here are some discoveries the children made about the illustrations in the picture books we read:

- Sometimes art fills the whole page (Andrew) from *Scarecrow*
- Sometimes the pictures are outlined in one color so the picture "pops" (Leo) from *Scaredy Squirrel*
- Picture matches words (Grace) from *Low Song*
- Sometimes illustrators draw close-ups (Gabriel and Luke) from *Scaredy Squirrel Makes a Friend* and *Wolves*
- Sometimes different materials are used (Gabriela, Mark, Alex) from *Black Cat*, *It's a Dog's New York*, *Chickerella*
- Sometimes illustrators use patterns with color/black and white (Jamie) from *Imagine* (by Bart Vivian)
- Sometimes illustrator doesn't finish the picture on purpose (Jackson) from *The Undone Fairy Tale*
- Illustrators use lines and patterns to show movement (Cecilia) from *Being Friends*
- Sometimes illustrators show time passing (Yuya) from *The Burger and the Hot Dog* and *Swing Around the Sun*
- Sometimes illustrations show more important parts of the picture bigger and less important parts smaller (Haley) from *Hooray for Feet*
- Sometimes illustrators use borders to help the reader understand (Devin) from *Cassie's Word Quilt*
- Illustrators sometimes use words or talk bubbles in the illustrations (Griffin) from *Two Eggs Please* and *Lilly's Purple Plastic Purse*

After the Discoveries, Then What?

Throughout the day, there are multiple opportunities for teaching. You could find me teaching to my objectives in a whole-class lesson or share, a writing focus lesson before the workshop time, a conference during writing, or during the share at the end of a workshop period. If you listened closely, it's very possible that you would hear writing talk as we're playing with Legos in choice time, choosing a book during reading workshop, or walking outside for dismissal. That's the way writing should be. It should be fluid and ongoing, not confined to one hour during each school day.

My friend and brilliant reading expert Sharon Taberski encourages teachers across the country to provide young children with "comprehension facilitating experiences" (Taberski 2002). These are experiences where the language of comprehension is named and the strategies are demonstrated for the children, over and over again in reading times throughout the day. Sharon says that while children may not be ready to go off and use a particular comprehension strategy to support their reading at that particular moment, they will be provided multiple opportunities for practice and time to watch a fluent reader in action. This way, comprehension strategies and behaviors are named and explicitly demonstrated so that when the time is right, young children will use what they know to enjoy and build meaning from a text.

I like to think of my writing instruction in the primary grades in this way—giving my students multiple writerly experiences so that when the time is right for them, they will use—in their own writing—the strategies, author's techniques, craft, and structures that have been named and demonstrated for them.

In each of my teaching times, I might point out a specific craft, structure, or topic idea and present it to the children in this way: "Did you know that writers sometimes ____? You might want to try that in your writing today." Rest assured that not everyone tries the writing possibilities that we talk about. Not everyone needs the writing possibilities we talk about. Not everyone is ready to write using the writing possibilities we talk about. But everyone participates in the discussion about these writing possibilities. And every student recognizes that this talk is important for our growth as a class of writers. The children also know that they may one day take this lesson and draw from it—in their own time and in their own way.

Besides using the discoveries of the children from our genre-reading share times to plan lessons, I also take the work of the children and just spend time reading through it to see what common patterns emerge as well as what specific lessons would benefit specific writers.

In this study I created a chart while reading the rough drafts the children had produced during the first two weeks. This chart helped me to see the following:

- The kinds of topics that had emerged
- The current quality, content, and craft of each child's piece
- Possible teaching points for focus lessons or guided writing groups
- Questions for each writer that might guide our next conference

This chart helped me figure out my course for other important lessons and conversations in our study and helped me know how best to help individual writers as well as the whole class. In this close examination of the children's rough drafts, I focused only on the *writing*, and would look closely at the illustrations and how they supported the writing work the children had done at another time. What you'll find in Figure 8.2 is a chart I developed from just one day of looking through the students' rough draft folders. I don't look this closely and this intently at each child's writing folder every day, but I do make a point of reviewing the class work as a whole at least once every week.

As you will see in the chart, there are so many teaching possibilities that come from just looking at a class of writers' work *once*, and it's okay to use that one deep review of the writing to carry you through several weeks of teaching. We have to give ourselves permission for that or we will drive ourselves crazy with all the other curriculum demands along with our writing curriculum.

Let's talk first about topic selection. Three important points about topic choice emerge from the data in this chart. First, looking at the class as a whole, the children aren't "topic copiers" and their teacher certainly isn't a "prompt pusher." These children are autonomous and independent in their topic selection and know that choice for them is critical and necessary. For example, if you knew Leo and Yuya personally, you would know that these little guys are joined at the hip. They sit together in class, eat the same snack every day, and live on the monkey bars at recess together—but they chose different writing topics. After some trouble choosing a topic, Leo eventually decides to focus on his talking computer story, and Yuya is creating his own adaptation of an old kindergarten favorite, *There Was an Old Lady Who Swallowed a Fly*.

If you spent a little more time with this group, you would begin to call Haley, Cecilia, and Margaux the three blonde musketeers. These young authors talk on the phone and plan their pink outfits, have Cam Jansen book talks in reading workshop, and build collectively with Legos at choice time—but they chose different writing topics. Haley's creating the adventure of a curiously naughty cat. Margaux is taking her readers through the many moods of Louise the Ladybug, and Cecilia has created a family of fictional dog characters who Rollerblade, are regulars at the weekly yoga class, and get their paw nails manicured with glossy polish (pink, of course).

In each of these pieces, choice is respected. Choice is celebrated. Choice is not a privilege but a right with these primary writers.

Second, this group of young authors writes for a purpose and a specific audience. These students each have their own story to tell and are writing about what they've learned, what they love, and what they know for an audience that matters to them. According to Gigi Brusco, a kindergarten student, she's got the best big sister ever. Big sister Jamie happens to be in our class, and Jamie is writing about her interests as compared with the interests of her little sister.

Mrs. Mullen and the memorable experiences she created for her kindergarten students last year became Nan's reason to write. Nan is writing to honor Mrs. Mullen and the happy moments from kindergarten with "My Kindergarten Top Ten." Robby knows that every kindergarten student needs to learn the alphabet, and every kindergarten student likes to learn in exciting ways. He's combined letters, food, and fun to write a food alphabet book modeled from one of his favorites, *Fed Up* by Rex Barron. When I ask the question, "Who's your audience?" I don't get funny looks or hear the question, "What do you mean?" I get direct answers, sometimes a spontaneous read-aloud from the draft, and even a first-grade hug or two.

Fig. 8.2 In-Process Writing Chart

Name of Child	Topic of Piece	Title of Piece	Teaching Points	Questions/Discussion Topics for the Writer
Yuya	Adaptation of *There Was an Old Lady Who Swallowed a Fly*	"There Was an Old Baby Who Swallowed a Scorpion"	Listing/adding parts	How could you add to this piece using the pattern you've already developed?
Mark	Superhero	"What's That Up in the Sky?"	Trimming the shrubs	Is there anything that you could take out that would help the reader understand better?
Spencer	A man who keeps his town safe	"Sam the Sheriff"	Adding more—letting the reader in on the "mind story" or "inside story"	None
Grif	Skateboarding	"The Never-Give-Up Skateboarder"	Editing for spelling and punctuation	None
Leo	No topic chosen		Choosing best topic to pursue	Which story interests you (and would interest readers)?
Grace	Animals	"Active Animals"	Lifting the content and quality of the writing	How can we make this book both fiction and nonfiction to give readers more info?
Alex	Lions	"The Little Lion"	Story order—page numbers/puzzle pieces analogy	Have you ever tried to put a puzzle together without all the pieces?
Mimi	Sea animals counting book	Untitled	Spelling—adding words to the page	One repeating sentence to add content
Cecilia	Dogs	Untitled	Adding pieces to the puzzle	Give analogy of a puzzle—missing pieces

Fig. 8.2 In-process Writing Chart (continued)

Name of Child	Topic of Piece	Title of Piece	Teaching Points	Questions/Discussion Topics for the Writer
Haley	Cats	Untitled	Craft a blurb rather than introduction	Let's take a look at some blurbs in picture books.
Nan	Kindergarten memories	"My Kindergarten Top Ten"	Brainstorming for more/lists	Tell me more about your kindergarten favorites.
Margaux	Ladybugs	"Louise the Ladybug"	Following a pattern	What other feelings does your character feel?
Jeff	Cactus (fiction)	"Mr. Cactus and Jimmy Play Hide and Go Seek"	Use background knowledge to develop the setting	Could we do some research on the desert to make your piece "true"?
Kiki	Friends	Untitled	Setting up pages/planning structure for story	Can we divide your book into two parts? Let's work with the good friends part first.
Gabriel	Sharks and fish	"The Shark and His Little Fish Friend"	Choosing one story to focus on—not three within one	Which part of this sounds more interesting to you?
Luke	Snowboarding	Untitled	Inserting examples	What kinds of things do snowboarders do to practice?
Jackson	Soccer/football	Untitled	Dialogue heavy—sandwich without the meat analogy	Have you ever eaten a hamburger without the meat?
Robby	Food alphabet	Untitled	Spelling/adding a pattern of sentences	How can we make this a book that kindergartners can practice reading?
Jamie	Sisters	Untitled	Structure—creating an alternating effect	How can we lay this story out so it becomes a pattern for the reader? Kindergartners like patterns.
Andrew	No topic chosen		"Talking out" the story	None

The third important point about topic choice concerns titles. It's interesting to see the range of titles (or lack thereof) at this point in the study. I see students who have developed a sense of what a title should do—capture the reader's attention or give enough information to draw the reader in. The students with titles know that this part of a book is a signal for what's to come, that the title is a window into the story that's ahead.

Let's take a closer look at a few of the writers in my class during this study using the notes I made in the chart in Figure 8.2. After several days of rough draft work, Mark asked for a conference with me because he wanted to show me all his pages. Mark was writing a story about a superhero and had about thirty full pages of text when he greeted me with a bright smile that early writing morning in May. As you can imagine, these thirty pages of fiction writing weren't all connected to his topic, and Mark had moved from superhero story to superawful, going-nowhere-fast fiction. This was the day that the yellow highlighter became Mark's friend. Instead of throwing away all that unnecessary writing and sending this child off to work feeling defeated in his attempts to write a superhero story, I gave him a job—to be a "super-text-trimmer." Mark's job was to reread what he had written and highlight all parts that didn't include the superhero or the superhero's friends. (This was the first step in helping him weed out unnecessary, unconnected material.) Mark needed to make the choice of "to trim or not to trim," not me. I needed to give this young writer full responsibility in making his book the best it could be. It would be in follow-up conferences that I would gently insert a comment or suggestion, rather than taking the pen in my hand and crossing through all Mark's hard work. Our teaching point in his conference would be *Growing writers of fiction sometimes have to reread and weed out writing that doesn't connect to the topic or make the story better.*

Mark needed several (okay, *many*) conferences to truly understand what this meant to his piece of writing, but that didn't stop me from giving him that challenge and teaching point when I recognized what he needed. With lots of trust and support, Mark was able to write a full, well-connected fiction piece by the end of our study.

In another conference on that same day, I met with Leo. One of my strongest writers, Leo had started and stopped multiple pieces over the past few weeks. He had no idea what to pursue and had no stick-to-itiveness with this project. Unlike Mark's conference, where we were developing a strategy for removing excess writing, Leo's conference simply needed to be a reminder of how to get started with a piece. Many times, even at the end of a writing year, we have to go back to those first weeks of writing conferences—helping a writer find and stick with an idea. Luckily, with Leo, helping him make a list of his passions and expertise led him directly to his topic: computers. Leo knew lots about these machines and how they worked (and especially loved our computer lab time during the day), so he decided to write a piece about a talking computer! The teaching point in Leo's conference would be *When growing writers are stuck and can't think of an idea, it's sometimes helpful to make a list of things they love and know a lot about.* That list, that strategy for idea generating, was all Leo needed, and now he was well on his way to writing a very clever, humorous piece about a kid and his talking computer.

Looking at my chart, I see that Kiki needed a conference about organization, Grace needed one about lifting the quality of the writing and adding more information, Jackson needed support balancing dialogue with narration, and Robby and Mimi needed work with mechanics. Each of these students needed different teaching at a different time, and that's why it's important for me to chart out where children are in the writing journey—so that I can support them in the most appropriate conference at the most appropriate time in the writing study. The ending point is the same, but the way we get to the published pieces is completely individual. Every day of the study during independent writing and conference time, and every day during our share time, I am able to teach the writers what they need specifically, and they are able to teach me what they know and have learned about writing to this point in the year. See Appendix E for an example of a support sheet I might use with writers ready to publish their pieces.

These students know that their piece, their finished book, is just one more addition, one more step in their journey as a growing writer. The children know that the completion of this project is just one more representation in their body of work as writers this year. Before the children read and talk about these books with their kindergarten friends, they will be able to look closely at the work they've produced and compare it with their writing from the beginning of the year. These primary writers will see the drastic difference between end-of-year writing and the writing they celebrated at that first publishing party back in October. The children will see growth, and they will feel it in their hearts and hands as they turn the pages of old and new, beginning and ending pieces.

Titles like "What's That Up in the Air?" and "The Never-Give-Up Skateboarder" and "Mr. Cactus and Jimmy Play Hide and Go Seek" replace beginning-of-year titles like "The Dog," "The Boy," "The Skateboard." In these later picture books you'll find boldfaced words and exclamation marks and "zoomed-in" illustrations and color changes to show feeling. October books just say, "I'm sad. I'm happy." June words like *crunchy* and *chewy* and *gooey* and *deliciously baked* replace those October *good cookies*. In June the stories have characters that bring problems and solutions to life, unlike those beginning-of-year stories that are missing everything but "once upon a time."

Let it be clear that the writing every day from October to December to February to April paved the way for June's publication. Our writing journeys begin with little steps, and as we step forward we grow stronger in our writing lives. These final pieces show us that it's the steps we take along the way that are essential to reaching our destination. And as Nikki Grimes says in her poetry picture book, *Shoe Magic*, "What you do, where you go, who you grow up to be depends on the steps you take." The giant step will be when these young writers take the books they've written and read proudly to an audience of kindergarten classes and show their friends the journey they've taken to grow up as a writer, as a published author.

What I Learned "About the Authors"

Not only does the writing inside these books show what these first graders have learned about process, topic, format, and craft this year, but the author's notes on the back of each book tell me a great deal more. I learn not just about the writing, but about the *writers* who worked so hard these last few months to produce such gorgeous picture books for their kindergarten peers. (See Figures 8.3 and 8.4 for examples of these notes.)

Just looking at the author's notes from Jeffrey and Jamie and Devin and Cecilia, I know immediately from their words that these kids see themselves as writers—with a bit of a skewed

Fig. 8.3 Jamie's Notes About the Author

About The Author

My name is Jamie. I am six years old. I wrote about me and my sister Gigi and I've writtin about rainbows and flowers. I've been writing for six years now and it is fun. You should try it. My favorit food is cake and cupcakes and ice cream and cookies and pancakes and soup and fish and meet and cheese, and webkinz.

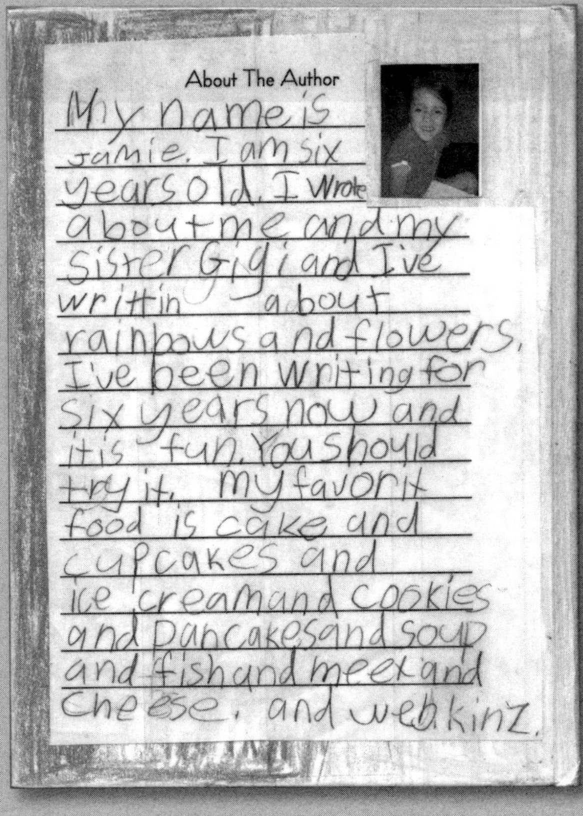

Fig. 8.4 Devin's Notes About the Author

About The Author

Hi, my is Devin Portner. I am 7 years old. I made books called What I like How to make a smiley face Sea creatures and the Happy and Sad book. I have been writing non-fiction fiction and Poetry. I wrote this book becuse I like ladybugs. I have been writing for 3 years. My next plan is to tell the Top Ten Things About First Grade.

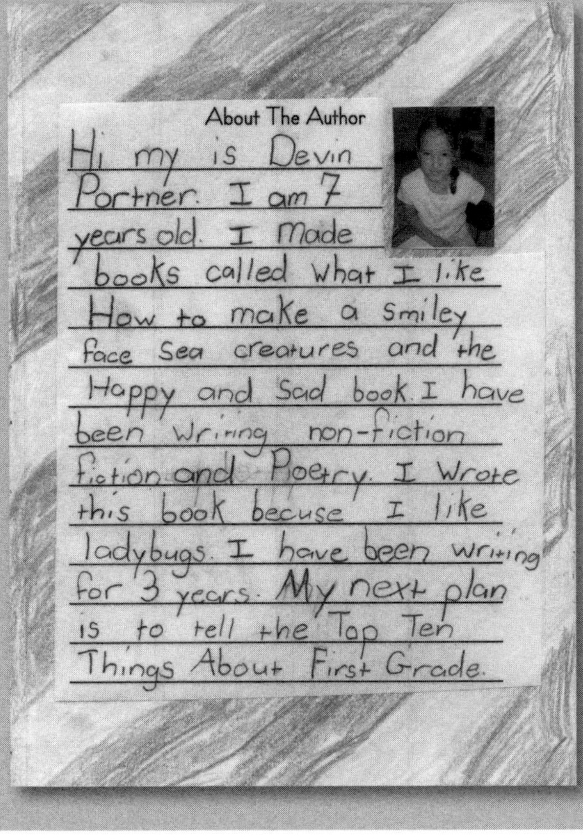

time line of how long they've actually been putting pen to paper. Jeffrey, Cecilia, and Devin are sure they've been authors for at least three or four years (of the six full years of their lives). Jamie tells us "I'm six years old… I've been writing for six years now and it is fun. You should try it." Jamie can't imagine her life without writing, and although these children are only six and seven, each one believes that writing is something they've done "for years" and something they will continue to do for a long time.

In the "about-the-author" pages, we learn of previous pieces they've published—in every genre and topic imaginable—from rainbows and flowers to sea creatures and smiley faces in poetry, fiction, and nonfiction. Significant amounts of time have been devoted to topic selection, drafting, revising, conferring, sharing, celebrating, and lots and lots of daily writing so that these children could produce multiple publications in multiple genres.

Not only do we get a sense of their previous writing work, but we also learn about their plans for future writing. Their plans have nothing to do with what's being assigned next in school. The children wrote their author pieces in June, with less than two weeks left in the school year—and at that point had internalized the understanding that writers write for audiences and purposes inside *and outside* of the school setting (and simply because it's something they love to do!). Jeffrey plans to create the second book in his Mr. Cactus and Jimmy series: "Mr. Cactus and Jimmy Pirates Ahoy!" Devin's looking to write about her top ten memories from first grade, and Cecilia "will write poetry next… Bye!" Writing is a huge part of their lives, but we also see the other important parts of their lives shining through: pets (that they love or even despise), big brothers and sisters, and "cake and cupcakes and ice cream and cookies and pancakes and soup and fish and meat and cheese and Webkinz"!

It's clear that these children have become authors who write with a plan, a purpose, and a sincere passion for the subject. They have grown in ways that I would never have imagined back in September. But with a daily writing routine, focused and specific teaching, and time to practice, talk, and share, these children were able to write and publish quality pieces and celebrate what they know about the subject. Remember, when teaching writing, it's not the writing curriculum that matters most—it's the fact that your work should be all about the authors. See Appendix E for a blank About the Author form.

Chapter 9
Publishing Possibilities
Tips and Techniques for Sharing, Showcasing, and Celebrating Student Writing

Publishing means many things to many writers and writing teachers. To me, publishing simply means "going public" with your writing. Publishing—and the celebration that goes along with it—is one giant step in our process, and possibly the most important part for children. For one, it's the first time for others (besides class and teacher) to read, honor, and respond to student writing. The pieces go forth into the world and become a representation of the reading, topic selecting, conferring, rough drafting, editing, revising, talking, sharing, rewriting, and reflecting work that we do across the days and weeks of a study. So much teaching and learning about writing is held in those pieces, and that writing deserves an audience and a celebration.

Although we typically think of publishing coming at the end of a writing study, it doesn't always have to happen that way. In the past I had always invited others in to see only those beautifully illustrated, perfectly spelled, content-filled, "perfect" pieces of writing. I realized one day that it was more than important—it was critical—that parents and administrators see the messiness: the thinking, the goal-setting, the misspelled words, the uncertainties about finishing, the word-starved pieces of paper. It was then that our class began hosting "in-process" celebrations, for parents, colleagues, administrators, and other students—sharing our work in the middle of a study. Adults need to see that writing is difficult and that the children worked long, hard, and purposefully day in and day out to move toward that goal they had set for themselves on the first day of the study—to publish a piece of writing for an audience in the hopes of evoking laughter, sparking curiosity, changing policy, creating hope, and filling the world with words that matter, words that beg to be read.

An in-process publishing celebration shows courage and gives the message that you believe in the writers in your care and that you have a strong vision of what's to come. I'm an advocate for those kinds of publishing celebrations as much as I'm a believer in end-of-study celebrations.

In this chapter you'll find some tips and techniques for publishing work through the year, when you're ready to showcase student work in the classroom, in the hallway, or in the world outside school. You'll find our materials list for each publication and tips or steps the children took to carry these pieces to completion.

I believe that the young writer's artwork and the way he or she showcases a piece of writing for an audience is as much a part of the writing process as the writing itself. So, in all of our publishing possibilities that follow, you'll find opportunities for students to not only write but illustrate, paint, color, cut, glue, and do all those artistic things that young children love to do.

Self-portrait Collages

At the beginning of the year, during our Establishing the Writing Community study, the children and I do lots of talking about what it means to be a writer and the kinds of work writers do in preparation for publishing a piece. Oral storytelling is a big part of our work as writers in the first few weeks, and getting the children to talk about their stories and lives is the first step in helping them become writers. The self-portrait collage is a great way to get this talk out into the room while also publishing a piece of artwork that becomes the springboard for more talk and writing. Typically during the first week of school, before the children create their self-portrait collage, I send a letter home to families asking for help in collecting items for the collage. These self-portrait collages hang at the top of a long wall or bulletin board that's out of reach for regular use in the room for the entire year.

I like to say to the children after the self-portrait collages are hung that our room is "wrapped in writers." That's the way a writing classroom should be—one that's wrapped in the work, the ideas, the thinking, and the lives of the children that inhabit the space. This year we added an extra touch to the self-portraits, with each child painting his or her name in bubble letters, outlined in thick black rope or yarn. I got this idea from my friend Kendall Fousak, a fabulous art teacher at Bronxville Elementary School in New York. Using the thick black yarn is an amazing way to highlight the children's names, rather than just having them outline their work in black marker. It gives each child's name texture and depth and really says, "Hey, look at me!" from the walls in our classroom.

Materials Needed

- Photographs of the child, child's family, special moments, and so forth
- Magazine or newspaper cutouts of pictures or words that describe the child, represent an interest or a hobby, or connect to their lives in some way
- Cray-Pas, oil pastels, watercolor, tempera paint, crayons (whichever medium you or the child chooses for the portrait will depend on your access to supplies and the depth of your patience for the day!)
- Cups or plates and brushes if paint is used
- Newsprint to cover tables
- Paper towels and spray cleaner for cleanup

- White butcher paper/bulletin-board paper
- Black fadeless paper
- Scissors
- Glue sticks
- Fabric glue
- Fabric or yarn
- Black cording or thick black yarn
- Skin-colored paints, markers, or crayons
- Photograph of the child's face and upper body

Tips and Techniques

☆ I first demonstrate how I would draw my self-portrait, giving the students a sense of how to begin, how big to make the portrait, and what details to add. I ask the children to first sketch their face and upper body using *whisper writing*—a term I learned from my friend Joan Backer at Manhattan New School—which involves writing lightly with a pencil and makes erasing easier and less messy. We work lots on drawing *big* so that filling in the pictures with color is much easier and more attractive. I also show the students examples of what not to do if they want people to see the portrait and for it to show up on the walls in our classroom.

☆ After the children sketch their self-portrait, it's time to decorate using color. The media you choose is up to you. One year, my students used Cray-Pas and oil pastels for their faces and tempera paint for their T-shirts. This year, my students first outlined their face, hair, features, and T-shirt with black permanent marker and then colored over it with crayon. (It's important when using crayons and permanent markers to use the marker first, since they don't work well over waxy crayon.)

☆ Hair—The children then either paint their hair color with washable tempera or acrylic paint or use yarn and glue the hair around the face with fabric glue.

☆ Young children have an easier time making the details of their faces with skinny permanent markers. Once the face is painted or colored with the appropriate skin color and is dry, then the students add the details.

☆ Once the entire portrait is dry, the children then paste pictures, words, cutouts, and so forth. on the T-shirt part of the body.

☆ This year, we added an extra step to the project, painting our names in bubble letters and then outlining the names with fabric glue and thick black yarn. I used acrylic paint this year. It's much brighter and doesn't fade as much as regular tempera paint or watercolors. But make sure your kids wear painting T-shirts or smocks. Acrylic paint is stubborn and can ruin clothes!

☆ After finishing the collages, the next two weeks of writing share is devoted to two or three children talking each day about their self-portraits and the meanings and stories behind the pictures and words on the collage. This share time is the perfect support for helping us begin to talk and write about our experiences and for us all to learn about the members of our classroom community. It also gives me a talking point when I have those first writing conferences of the year and still need to remind the children of their experiences and how those experiences can become ideas for writing. (See Figure 9.1 for examples of these self-portrait collages.)

Fig. 9.1 Self-Portrait Collages

Poetry Posters

One way to publish the poetry of young children, rather than in book form, is by creating a "poetry poster." These are large-sized (half of a regular poster paper) publications, and are an incredible way to add life, color, and quality writing to the halls of your school or classroom. It's a way for audiences across the school (or outside the school) to see and read the work of young poets. I believe it's important for children's work to stand out. I've been known by fellow colleagues as the teacher who works and publishes in "oversized" mode. The bigger the better, right? With my big-as-life philosophy, the poetry poster idea was born.

Materials Needed

- White posterboard or large sheets of white watercolor paper or oversized white card stock
- Pencils (Dixon Ticonderoga #1 or #2 are best.)
- Cups for water
- Paper towels for cleanup and for dabbing brushes
- Crayola watercolors (the larger multipacks with extra colors are best), tempera paint, or acrylic
- Paintbrushes (large and small sizes)
- Fine-tip and medium-tip black permanent markers
- Bright card stock or construction paper
- Lined paper for writing
- Scissors for cutting patterns on edges (optional)
- Photo paper for author photo
- Fadeless paper for mounting

Tips and Techniques

☆ When beginning the poster, I typically ask my students to sketch an illustration that would support the words in their poem first, in pencil (on the blank, oversized paper). As with the self-portrait collages, I like to tell the children to use whisper writing, since it makes erasing easier and less messy. We work lots on drawing *big*. This makes filling in the pictures with color much easier, and it looks attractive.

☆ After the picture or illustration for the poem is sketched in pencil, children begin painting. I've also found that it's helpful, if the children are writing their poem onto the poster, for them to write in pencil and then draw a bubble around the writing so that when it's time to paint, words don't get painted over. Before we paint, I always demonstrate the use of the medium we are using *first* to avoid any paint catastrophes and six-year-old breakdowns. If we use watercolors, I show the students that more water equals lighter colors and less water equals darker colors. I also emphasize that watercolor is not an exact science—colors will mix and bleed and that is okay! It makes the work even more beautiful. With acrylic or tempera paint, it's important to help children recognize that this is more of an exact, stay-in-the-lines type of painting—or you will wind up with "garbage-can colors" if lots of mixing occurs.

☆ Backgrounds are important, so most of the time I ask the children to choose a background color and fill in all the white space instead of leaving only the main illustration painted. Colored backgrounds make for bold, stunning pieces.

☆ We always allow for a paint drying time, and then the children outline their drawing with either fine- or medium-tipped permanent markers. This black outline helps the picture say, "Look at me!" (It's also nice to mat the picture with black fadeless paper. It gives a nice, professional look and allows the color of the child's work to stand out.)

☆ If you're interested in giving the piece a bit of texture, students can write their final draft poems on lined paper and then back that writing with colored card stock. This paper-to-card-stock mounting also makes the writing stand out on the background art.

☆ Many times either the children or I choose an interesting font that matches their topic or reflects the mood of the piece, and we type the title, author, and illustrator. That extra-bold, extra-large title is cut out and mounted on the background art.

☆ Sometimes I help the children cut around their piece with decorative scissors to give the piece an interesting border before mounting it on the fadeless paper.

☆ Ta da! Now your children have fabulous writing and gorgeous art to enhance the published piece! (See Figure 9.2 for an example of a poetry poster.)

Class Poetry Anthology

As a final poetry project a few years back, my students and I put together a class poetry anthology. Included in this poetry anthology were typed copies of each child's poem. This project provided an authentic way to showcase the final pieces of an entire class of young

Fig. 9.2 Poetry Poster

poets, and this book was a great gift for parents, administrators, and students at the end of the study. Long after the poetry study was over, students, teachers, and family members returned to this anthology on the shelves of classrooms, offices, and home libraries. The anthologies I've since created with other classes have also been a great model for new classes and new students as we begin the next year's poetry study. Children learn lots from the writing of their peers, and this book houses class sets of writing by former students of equal age to my new class of students.

Materials Needed

- White copy paper (8 ½" X 11")
- Glossy photo paper
- Computer, digital camera, printer
- Scissors
- Glue sticks
- Pencils
- Fine-tip permanent markers
- Crayons
- Colored card stock (enough for the entire class to have a front and back cover on each individual book)
- Plastic ring binding/binding machine
- Clear plastic presentation covers (to protect the front and back covers of the anthology)
- Color copier (or class donation money to make color copies at local copy center)

Tips and Techniques

☆ Depending on the age of your students, their proficiency with word processing, or the time you've allotted to this project, you make the decision whether students type their poems or someone else—a parent volunteer, teaching assistant, or teacher—does the typing.

☆ It's visually interesting and more appealing to the eye of the reader when every poem is typed in a different font—or a font that matches the mood, tone, or feeling of the piece. It also gives each child more ownership and adds a touch of original quality to each piece.

☆ Before putting the poems together in book form, each child is given the final typed piece of his or her poem. Since color copying is so expensive, I ask the children to illustrate their pieces like the pictures in a coloring book. We first draw in whisper writing, and then the children outline their pencil drawing in black fine-tip permanent markers (so that the illustrations will show clearly on each poem when copied).

☆ Not only do the children have a typed poem for the anthology, they have also previously published this same exact poem on a poetry poster to hang in the school. This poster was illustrated with watercolor and oil pastels.

☆ In the years I've made the poetry anthology with students, I've simplified the project a bit, and rather than writing completely new poems, the students used previously published poetry to be included in the anthology. It's up to you and your class of students to decide whether you'll use the same poems published as poetry posters or create entirely new poems for an anthology.

☆ Through class fund money or parent donations (or me saying it'll be a tax write-off and paying for the copies myself), we are able to make a color copy of the cover for each child's anthology.

☆ After enough copies of the book are made so that each individual student will have his or her own copy, they are bound using the school binding machine with plastic ring binding (found at most office supply stores).

☆ Each child then has an opportunity to add color inside to each poem or to just a few selected poems. Their color choices for the inside poems make each child's book unique and personal.

The color insert shows the collage cover of a poetry anthology.

Nonfiction Did You Know...? Bubbles

I noticed that each day during our nonfiction genre study, several students would always discover and want to share the amazing facts highlighted in bubbles and boxes—or what the children began to call Did You Know…? Bubbles in the texts they were reading. These parts of the nonfiction texts we read always contained intriguing or amazing information, and the idea for this next type of publication format came from my students' interest in the Did You Know…? Bubbles. Since nonfiction text is so dense and content filled, it's a bit daunting to tackle a writing project that necessitates a large amount of text with a group of primary students. It was obvious to me that the children were totally interested in the genre, but I needed to provide a way for them to publish their new knowledge and learning about topic and genre in a way that wasn't so text heavy. We studied nonfiction text features and how those features help the reader understand, and we showcased this knowledge of topic and text features by publishing our very own Did You Know…? Bubbles. The writing in this publication was fact-filled but less intimidating and time consuming than writing a multipage book on a nonfiction topic. It was a great scaffold into the deeper, longer work with nonfiction the students would do later in the year and in the years to come.

In keeping with my bigger-than-life philosophy for publishing, these pieces were big! To create the bubble effect, I used the bottom of a large, round garbage can to trace the circles onto white posterboard or butcher paper.

Materials Needed

- One piece of posterboard for each student
- Round garbage can or large, round bin for tracing the circle onto the posterboard
- Watercolors or oil pastels
- Colored pencils
- Black fine-tip permanent markers
- Nonfiction text feature templates
- Scissors
- Glue sticks

Tips and Techniques

☆ I first share with the class an example of a Did You Know…? Bubble that I created from our whole-class study of spiders. (See Figure 9.3.) The children and I have been reading books together as I model the process for nonfiction research, note taking, and sharing that nonfiction knowledge, so I make sure I model how that research and note taking transfers to a final, published piece.

☆ Students first trace and cut each piece of posterboard into a circle or "bubble." In the past I've simply left the posterboard square, but the circular shape seemed to make the most sense because it grew out of the actual Did You Know…? Bubbles in the texts we were reading.

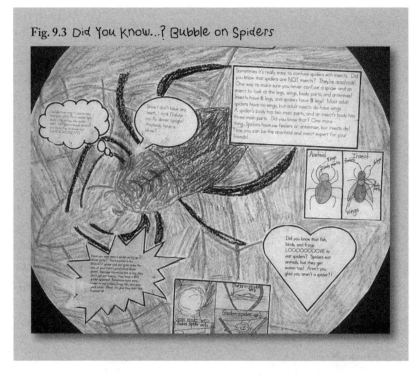

Fig. 9.3 Did You Know...? Bubble on Spiders

☆ After tracing and cutting out the bubbles, the students then work on the background, using either watercolor to fill in or oil pastels to represent their topics. For example, Erin and Caitlin chose to paint their background yellow-orange with black spots to frame their writing about the cheetah. Miles painted his background blue with a trickle of red running through it to represent the ocean water and the blood from the prey of the shark he researched. My background was a giant spider on his web with a sky-blue background. In each of these projects, the illustrations and background color gives life and purpose to the writing around it.

☆ Next, the students choose the nonfiction text-feature templates that would best showcase their research. Some students might choose the square boxes to draw and label diagrams. Others might choose the long, skinny text boxes to use as captions under illustrations. A heart might show up on the poster signifying this animal's favorite foods or habitat.

☆ After the students have written and illustrated and colored their information in the text-feature template boxes, they then place the information on the bubble in a clear and organized way. (No glue-sticking until all parts are in the proper place or we've got a mess on our hands!)

☆ Once students have glued all information onto the bubble, it's time to add the finishing touches. Outlining illustrations, captions, or diagrams in fine-tip black permanent marker helps the research stand out. (Figure 9.4 shows a final student Did You Know…? Bubble.)

Fig. 9.4 Bryce's Did You Know...? Bubble

How-To Books

Procedural writing is another nonfiction writing study I've pursued with students in the past. We typically learn about this type of writing after our study of nonfiction features and after the students have a strong grasp of the variety of nonfiction texts in the world (and in our classroom). We publish how-to books to teach our readers—anything from how to build a birdhouse to how to make a banana split to how to be a great best friend. The books are half the size of a regular 8½ X 11–inch sheet of paper, so that students will have more pages in their books and will truly separate their information into a step-by-step format. They're small, perfect for small hands, and look completely different from any other publishing format we've used in previous studies.

Materials Needed

- Colored card stock (preferably colors that match the illustrations in the piece or connect to the writer's topic)
- How-to template paper
- Pencils
- Glue sticks
- Paper cutter
- Black permanent markers
- Colored pencils
- Cover and title page template paper
- Plastic ring binding
- Clear presentation cover sheets (for protecting book cover)
- Opaque presentation cover sheets (for protecting book end page)

Tips and Techniques

☆ For this publication we use heavy, bright card stock for the cover, interior, and end pages. The children then glue their writing onto this card stock when it's completed and in order.

☆ We typically cover the front and back covers with clear presentation sheets and bind them together with a plastic ring binding machine. This type of binding with the clear cover gives them a polished, professional, gorgeously published look.

☆ So that the children can make sure that all steps in their how-to book are in order and placed exactly where they should go, the children don't actually write on the colored card stock background. They cut out and glue their steps/writing inside the book when they're finished writing. This helps us avoid "Oh no! I wrote the wrong step on the wrong page!" or "I messed up! I need to do the whole thing over now!"

☆ Before everything is glued inside, we reread, edit, revise, and place the writing in the correct order so the reader will be able to understand.

☆ Either before or after gluing writing inside the book, the children outline their writing in fine-tip black permanent marker and color illustrations with colored pencils (also outlined in black marker). A blank writing support sheet for How-To ideas, a blank writing reflection sheet for How-To writing, and How-To template paper can be found in Appendix D. Examples of How-To writing are on pages 119–120.

Content-Area Museum Displays (Birds of New York City Study)

This final writing/art project was actually created during a content-area study rather than during the actual writing workshop period. I'm including it here because my students used their knowledge of nonfiction writing and illustrating with a variety of media (all from our work in writing workshop) to produce this museum display for our science study of bird habitats in New York City. At the time of this study, I was lucky to live in a classroom at the Manhattan New School that was once the old library. Entire sides of two walls in the classroom were covered with built-in bookcases. Instead of filling each bookcase with books, we reserved one entire section of shelves to create the New York City birds museum display. Even if you don't have a wall of bookshelves that can be emptied, it's still possible to create this type of project with shoe boxes, small wooden craft boxes, or even bigger packing boxes—depending on your display, room arrangement, and purpose for the project.

This class of second graders had first read and studied lots of books about birds and birds native to New York City. We then visited the Metropolitan Museum of Art to study the way that artifacts and museum displays were written about—on name plates and plaques beside each piece of art or display. Our work toward this publishing celebration was twofold—to study the writing of museum plaques and nameplates and to re-create a visual display that matched the writing we crafted for that particular display.

Materials Needed

- Empty bookshelves, rectangular cardboard boxes, solid rectangular wooden crates
- Digital camera
- Glossy photo paper
- Newspaper, flour, and water for papier-mâché
- Bowls for papier-mâché mix (number of bowls depends on number of groups of students working at a time)
- Multicolored tissue paper packs
- Materials to create a specific landscape (We used small Styrofoam balls, twine, pipe cleaners, colored construction paper, aluminum foil, fabric scraps, sand, small rocks, leaves, and tinted plastic wrap to create our bird habitats.)
- Fishing line
- Glue sticks
- Duct tape
- Fabric glue
- Colored card stock
- Museum plaque/nameplate template

Tips and Techniques

☆ The display plaque, teaching our readers and museum visitors about a particular bird habitat, was typed on colored paper, laminated, and mounted inside the bookshelf, alongside the display.

☆ Students used a variety of media to create their bird habitat. All birds were sculpted out of aluminum foil and newspaper and then taped together with masking tape to form a mold.

☆ The mold was then covered in papier-mâché and painted with acrylic paint when dry.

☆ Students researched actual bird and egg colors to make the display as authentic as possible.

☆ They then used mixed media, combining their own illustrations, craft materials, and photos taken from the actual habitat in the city to re-create those habitats.

☆ This project lasted several weeks, through many science periods, and became a reality because of the foundation we built during writing and reading workshop.

These children learned to be nonfiction writers by studying the genre and they became museum curators and docents, carefully crafting, creating, and teaching readers and visitors to our classroom about the birds of New York City. See Figure 9.5 for the habitat the children created for the great egret and the mallard duck.

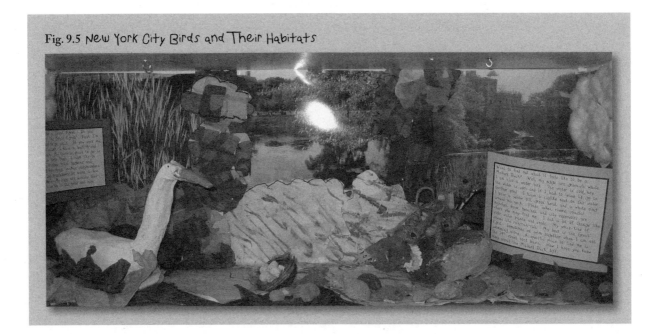

Fig. 9.5 New York City Birds and Their Habitats

Picture Books and Multigenre Flip Books

The Bare Book saved my life when students asked for a format "like the bookstore books" for their publications. I've spoken of these books in earlier chapters when I talked about the teaching point notebooks, but I cannot say how incredibly useful and beautiful they can become when filled with a child's words and illustrations. They, like the how-to publication I spoke of earlier, are filled with student writing and illustrations completed prior to assembling. Students cut their writing out so that it will fit on the blank pages, then place the writing and illustrations on each page, and finally glue them down in story order. The students create a cover illustration by either painting, using oil pastels, or markers to make their cover illustration "pop" and then glue it to the front of the book. I then cover the title and illustration with clear packing tape to secure the picture and provide that glossy, library-bound look. We use these books for our picture book and fiction/nonfiction comparison writing celebrations.

Materials Needed

- Bare Books (available from www.barebooks.com)
- Copy paper
- Markers, crayons, watercolors, or colored pencil (your students' choice of media for front and back book cover)
- Markers for outlining illustrations, writing, and details
- Glue sticks
- Laminating film/school laminating machine
- Clear packing tape with dispenser
- Picture book template paper
- Scissors
- About the Author template pages
- Digital photos of each child for author page
- Copyright and dedication template

Tips and Techniques

☆ I've found that using Bare Books is the best (and easiest) way for students to publish picture books or multipage writing projects. The books come in different sizes (with or without lines), are already bound like a real book, and are quite affordable. These books are now on my supply list at the beginning of each year, since I use them for the picture book and content-area publications as well as for the unit of study teaching point notebooks.

☆ I quickly realized that, with young children, problems—"Oops I messed up! May I have another piece of paper?!"—always happen when publishing. To avoid these problems, I learned to have the children glue on their cover pages and their writing and illustrations in the Bare Book *after* completing that work. It relieves us of the angst of getting it right the first time (something that writers *never* do anyway!).

☆ Writing and illustrating on separate paper and then gluing inside the book also allows the children to have more control over the organization, pace, or tension in the story. Even if the child has written the entire piece on one or two pages of copy paper, it's easy to then cut and paste in a way that helps the flow of the text or enables the child to stretch the story or information. This can happen by simply cutting apart sentences or pages and placing them on different pages in the Bare Book.

☆ The key is to leave the gluing until the very end. (It is not fun to try to carefully scrape a misplaced glued page off and then convince a child that it makes the work unique to have a big hole in the top of the illustration!)

☆ The children usually illustrate a cover page first in pencil and then color in marker or paint in watercolor or tempera paint. I've found that these pages become simply gorgeous when laminated or covered with clear packing tape.

☆ The children glue the cover page to the front of the book, and I then have either a parent volunteer or an assistant carefully wrap clear packing tape around the entire front cover to protect it from coming apart.

☆ A similar process is followed for the back cover, where the author's note appears. Once the author's note is completed, the student then glues a wallet-sized photo to the top of the page, which I then laminate. We glue the laminated page to the back and, as with the front cover, cover the whole thing with clear packing tape. Beautiful! Sturdy! Just waiting to be read! (See Figures 9.6 and 9.7 for samples of these book covers and interior pages.)

Fig. 9.6a Cover of Caitlin's Flip Book

Fig. 9.6b Sample Pages from Caitlin's Flip Book

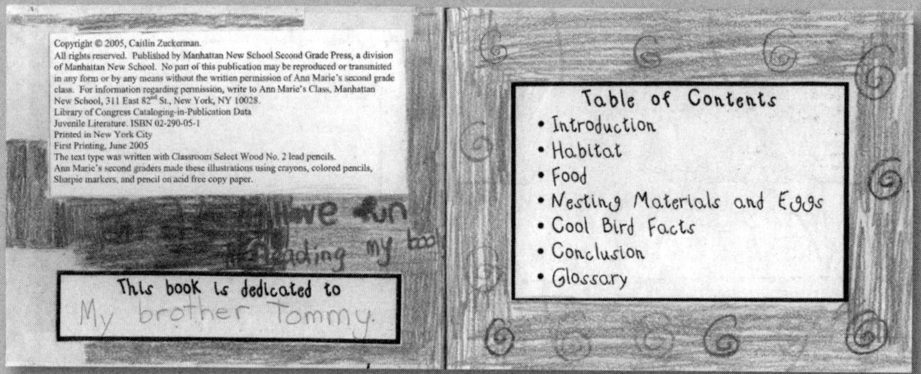

Copyright © 2005, Caitlin Zuckerman.
All rights reserved. Published by Manhattan New School Second Grade Press, a division of Manhattan New School. No part of this publication may be reproduced or transmitted in any form or by any means without the written permission of Ann Marie's second grade class. For information regarding permission, write to Ann Marie's Class, Manhattan New School, 311 East 82nd St., New York, NY 10028.
Library of Congress Cataloging-in-Publication Data
Juvenile Literature. ISBN 02-290-05-1
Printed in New York City
First Printing, June 2005
The text type was written with Classroom Select Wood No. 2 lead pencils.
Ann Marie's second graders made these illustrations using crayons, colored pencils, Sharpie markers, and pencil on acid free copy paper.

This book is dedicated to
My brother Tommy.

Table of Contents
• Introduction
• Habitat
• Food
• Nesting Materials and Eggs
• Cool Bird Facts
• Conclusion
• Glossary

Giving young writers the tools for publishing and showcasing their work in grand and beautiful ways is one of the writing teacher's greatest gifts to her students. Publishing student work in ways such as this sends powerful messages to students. First of all, it says to them that their work matters and their voices and artwork have a rightful place in the world of school and beyond. Second, providing a variety of publishing possibilities for students sends the clear message that there will always be an audience for their work, and that work deserves to shine and speak to readers in powerful, colorful, and authentic ways. To publish with intention and to publish with the tools real writers and illustrators use is imperative if we are to "grow" young writers who write with purpose and who care deeply about and feel proud of the writing work they produce.

Fig. 9.7a Cover of Dasha's Flip Book

Fig. 9.7b Sample Pages from Dasha's Flip Book

Chapter 10
Conclusion
Growing Forward with Young Writers

When I think of Haley, I think of the words *joyfully serious*. She's the child who would choose school days over weekends, has moved through first grade with a permanent toothless grin, and began writing on day one with a serious commitment to the work ahead of her. Over her first-grade year, Haley wrote fiction, poetry, nonfiction, and her first picture book about a curiously sneaky cat. Looking across the year at her pieces, I see a child who learned to write for different purposes and different audiences. Haley's first piece was designed to entertain all "dog lovers." Her second publication of the year, a poem, was written to sit in between the work of two favorite poets, Rebecca Kai Dotlich and Douglas Florian. In our how-to writing study, Haley wrote to teach young artists how to draw a butterfly. And in our last study of the year, our picture book study, Haley's story developed out of a love for cats and the kindergarten friends she would read to at the final celebration.

From the absence of any punctuation in her first piece to the use of exclamation points and apostrophes and ellipses in her last, Haley learned the power of punctuation and how it affects the reader's comprehension and engagement. She titled her beginning-of-year piece about a dog "The Dog." But her end-of-year picture book about a cat wasn't just titled "The Cat." Instead, it became "The Trouble with Curiosity." You could find books about bees and butterflies in the nonfiction section of our library, but Haley expanded her classmates' view of nonfiction, by writing a bee riddle poem and her piece about how to draw a butterfly. Haley's writing journey folders were filled with rough drafts, writing reflections, and statements about her successes and challenges. Through each study, she engaged in all parts of the writing process and continues to grow because she left first grade loving to write, and she has a lifetime of growing and writing ahead of her. Figure 10.1 shows the cover of Haley's first piece; Figure 10.2, the cover of her end-of-year publication.

Now, perhaps you remember Mark from the chapter on our picture book study. He's a practicing magician, an aspiring secret agent, the youngest sibling of five, and he was one of the twenty-two writers in my first-grade classroom. If you could spend the day with Mark, you'd feel his almost supercharged energy, hear his nonstop conversations, watch his serious play, and wonder if any of my teaching (and behavior

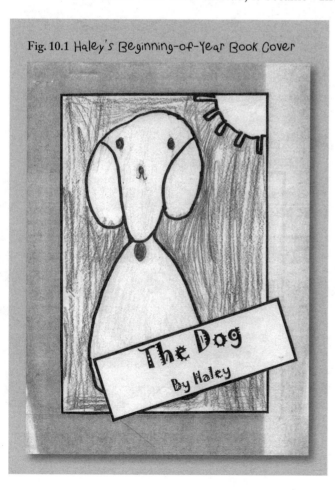

Fig. 10.1 Haley's Beginning-of-Year Book Cover

The Dog
By Haley

management techniques) was sinking in. He began the year drawing circle-eyed, stick-legged, neckless people and talked his way through stories, share times, and conferences. Mark is living, breathing proof that talk is a critical part of the young writer's growth. Mark's September and October work shows attempts at approximated spelling, beginning sentence structure, and the knowledge that people write about what they know and enjoy, as witnessed in his book "Things That Are Nice and Fun." This first piece has elements of one of our early read-alouds, *Do You Know What I'll Do?* by Charlotte Zolotow and this question and answer format shows up in this first publication. He also understands that we can learn to write from the authors we read.

Fig. 10.2 Haley's End-of-Year Book Cover

The Trouble With Curiosity

Meow!

Written and Illustrated by Haley Barr

Mark visits Häagen-Dazs regularly, and the ice-cream topic showed up in several places in his writing folder. He carried this recurring topic to publication at the December poetry party. "Yum! Yum," "frozen," "summer treat," "another word for good" were a few ways this poet described his ice cream. Mark's true passion and voice came out loud and clear in his piece "Shhhhh… How to Be a Secret Agent." According to Mark, if you want to be a secret agent, you'll need a gun, a belt, and gadgets. "Secret agents always use their brain." This aspiring secret agent knows how to entertain his readers, young and old alike. I so vividly remember those last few weeks of school when he was revising his final piece, "What's That Up in the Sky?" (Mark says this is the title because he didn't want to give away the topic and wanted to draw the reader inside.) I remember the multiple times I tried to coerce Mark to let go of his "more is more" idea with this thirty-page rough draft about a superhero. But for some reason, in one of my last conferences of the year with him, I needed to go a bit deeper than the lesson that more isn't necessarily more. That last month of school, I started his conference with the question, "What does this year's writing mean to you?" A big question for a little writer. A big question for a kid who fidgets with the pencil holder and organizes his papers as we talk. With a short pause, a deep breath, and a scratch of his chin, Mark replied, "Writing's like something that's a part of me. Something that I can't let go of. Like say… if I gave up writing for six or four days… it'd be like starting all over."

Fig. 10.3 Mark's Beginning-of-Year Writing

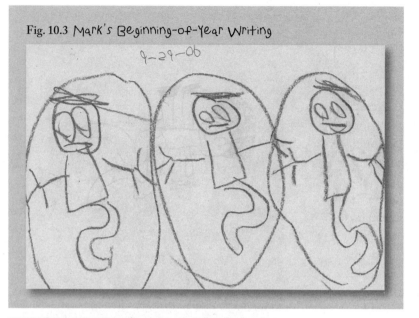

9-29-06

Fig. 10.4 Mark's End-of-Year Writing

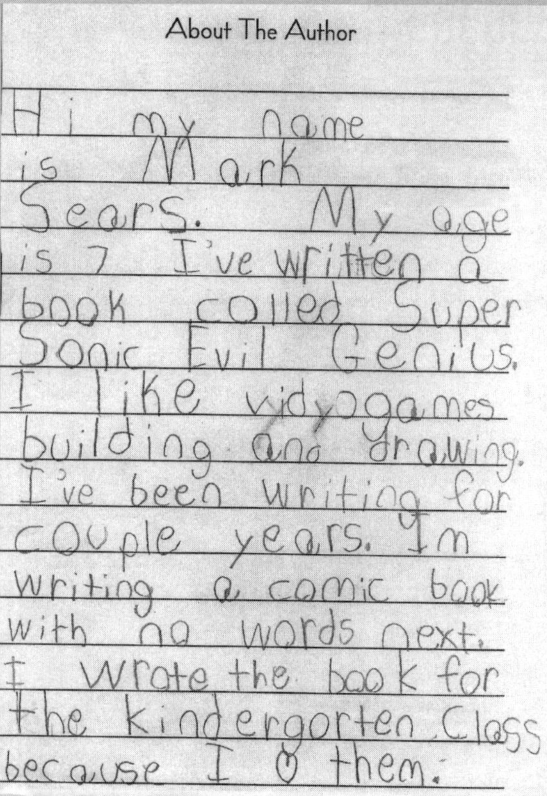

About The Author

Hi my name
is Mark
Sears. My age
is 7. I've written a
book colled Super
Sonic Evil Genius.
I like vidyogames
building and drawing.
I've been writing for
couple years. I'm
writing a comic book
with no words next.
I wrote the book for
the kindergorten class
because I ♡ them.

What a gift to learn after a year together that it's not just magic or recess or play dates or block building that he can't let go of. In that moment, Mark taught me the value of the writing work we'd done every day since that first day back in September. I learned that the year's writing work had become a part of the person he is. Mark won't ever have to start from scratch again, but will just continue to grow and write happily ever after. In Figure 10.3 you'll find Mark's first piece of writing in first grade. Figure 10.4 shows his About the Author piece in his final first-grade publication.

It's young writers like Haley and Mark who've taught me what's essential in being a teacher of writing. It's young writers like these who have taught me the importance of…

ANALYZING the writing plans and writing work and writing environment

ASKING and answering the hard questions

APPLAUDING the big and small writing steps

ASSISTING each other in the learning process

ASSESSING the work and the value of that work, and

ADVOCATING for children to always be a part of exemplary writing instruction

The child's growth as a writer and as a person. That's *of primary importance.*

The Year

By William

First I was scared
now I am not.
I didn't like reading
now I treat it as a friend.
When we started writing, That is what I was
worst at.
now I'm an author of a book.
From the first of this year leard
So much.
Now the year is ending.
Now it is time to leave
to a new year
again and again Forever

Appendix A
Record Sheets for Writers

Name_____ Week _____

Writing Record

<u>Monday</u>
Title/Topic _____

_____

<u>Tuesday</u>
Title/Topic _____

_____

<u>Wednesday</u>
Title/Topic _____

_____

<u>Thursday</u>
Title/Topic _____

_____

<u>Friday</u>
Title/Topic _____

_____

Genre Boxes
Red-Fiction   Blue-Nonfiction   Yellow-Poetry

Source: This form is adapted from a form in Sharon Taberski's book *On Solid Ground: Strategies for Teaching Reading K–3*. 2000. Portsmouth, NH: Heinemann.

Comments from My Readers

Name	Comment

Appendix B
Support Sheets for Establishing a Writing Community

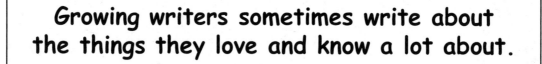

Growing writers sometimes write about
the things they love and know a lot about.

My Writing Journey
Our First Publishing Celebration

Author _____   Date _____

1. The rough draft title of my first published piece is
_____. My new title,
revised to grab the reader's attention, is
_____.

2. My piece shows that growing writers sometimes write
_____.

3. Some of my friends wrote about_____
_____.

4. I am most proud of_____
_____.

5. I would like to work to get better at_____
_____.

6. The purpose of my published piece is to _____
_____.

Comments from My Readers

Reader	Comments

Appendix C
Poetry Study Support Sheets

Poetry Visualization Support Sheet

Growing writers sometimes start a rough draft
with a visualization instead of with words.
(They illustrate poetry before writing it.)

A Rough Draft of My Visualization

Poetry Puzzle/Organization Support Sheet

Sometimes writers of poetry need to reorganize the words in their rough draft so that the poem both **looks and sounds** like poetry.

Name_____ Date_____

20/20 Words Support Sheet

When creating a piece, growing writers of poetry are very careful about their word choice. They work to use "20/20" words and not blurry words.

20/20 Words	Blurry Words
buttery	yellow
hilarious	funny

My Writing Journey
Poetry Study

Name_____ Date_____

- The topic of my poem is_____

- I chose to write a poem about this topic because _____
  _____
  _____

- Some of my friends wrote about_____
  _____
  _____

- I learned that poets think about these things when writing for
  their readers: _____
  _____
  _____

- These are some of the types of poems we discovered in our poetry
  reading each day: _____
  _____
  _____

- My top three favorite poetry books from this study are_____
  _____
  _____
  _____

- The thing I feel most proud of about my work in this study is
  _____
  _____
  _____

- The thing I'd like to work harder on next time is_____
  _____
  _____
  _____

Poetry Rough Draft Paper

Name_____ Date_____

Poetry Rough Draft Paper

Name_____   Date_____

_____

- -

_____

- -

_____

- -

_____

- -

_____

- -

_____

- -

_____

- -

_____

Appendix D
Nonfiction Study Support Sheets

Nonfiction Writing Support Sheet: Titles

Growing writers of nonfiction sometimes create a title for their readers that:

1. Teaches the reader a tidbit about the topic in the main title ("Silk Spinners")
2. Has a subheading that tells the reader the main topic of the piece ("Let's Learn About Spiders")
3. May have the sound of "poetic" words that are catchy to the eye and ear ("Ssss... Ssss...")

My Rough Draft Title Possibilities

1. _____

_____

_____

_____

2. _____

_____

_____

_____

3. _____

_____

_____

_____

Nonfiction Writing Support Sheet: Organization

After thinking of a topic, growing writers of
nonfiction sometimes choose the specific parts of the topic
they will research before writing a rough draft.

Name_____ Date _____

My Topic

_____

Possible suheadings, subtitles, or parts of this topic that I will include in my rough draft:

1._____

2._____

3._____

4._____

My Writing Journey
Nonfiction Features Study

Name_____ Date_____

1. _____ was the topic I researched
and wrote about in this writing study.

2. During this study we learned to take meaningful notes from nonfiction texts.
These are some important tips I learned about taking notes: _____
_____
_____

3. In this study we learned about nonfiction features and how they help the
reader. These are some of the features I learned about and what they're used
for in nonfiction texts:
a._____
_____
b._____
_____
c._____
_____
d._____
_____
e._____
_____
f._____
_____
g._____
_____

4. As I was reading and writing, I learned lots about my topic. This is some
important and interesting information I learned about _____:
_____
_____

5. I feel most proud of these parts of my Did You Know... ? Bubble writing project:
_____
_____

6. These are a few things I feel I could do even better in my next writing project:
_____
_____

Nonfiction Rough Draft Paper

Name_____ Date_____

Writing Support Sheet
Ideas for How-To Texts

Name _____ Date _____

What could I teach my readers?

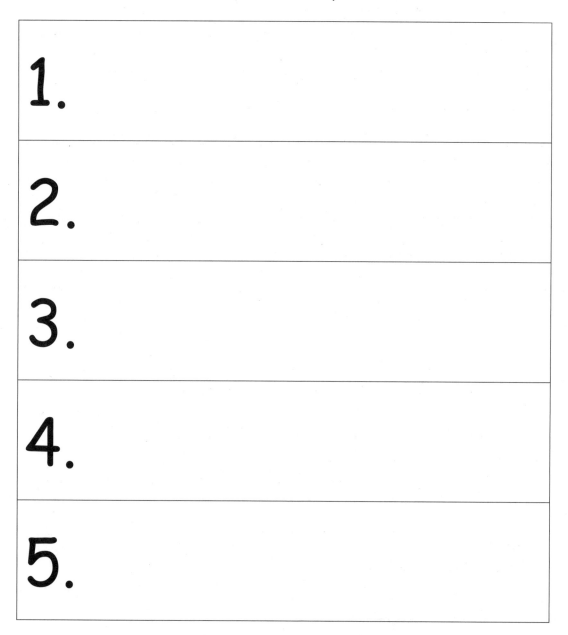

1.

2.

3.

4.

5.

My Writing Journey Reflection
Procedural/How-To Writing Study

Name _____ Date_____

1. The first draft title for my how-to piece was _____
_____, but then I wanted to make sure I captured the reader's attention,
so I changed my title to_____.

2. Last year's second-grade authors inspired our writing and gave us ideas for our
own pieces. This was the book that helped me most:
_____ by_____.

3. This book gave me these ideas for my own writing: _____
_____

4. The purpose of writing how-to pieces is to _____
_____.

5. These are a few ways I made sure my introduction captured the reader's
attention so they would read on and learn about my topic: _____
_____
_____

6. These are two things I learned that are extremely important when writing
how-to pieces: 1._____
2._____

7. How-to pieces can be pretty "blah" to read unless a writer adds his or her own
creative touch to the writing. Here's an example from my writing of how I wrote
with voice and personality: _____
_____

8. As an experienced how-to writer, I am most proud of _____
_____

9. If I had this study to do over or if I revisit this kind of writing next year, I'd
like to get better at _____
_____

10. My favorite part of this study was_____

Here's my autograph when I become a famous writer or illustrator one day!

Author's Signature _____

How-To Paper

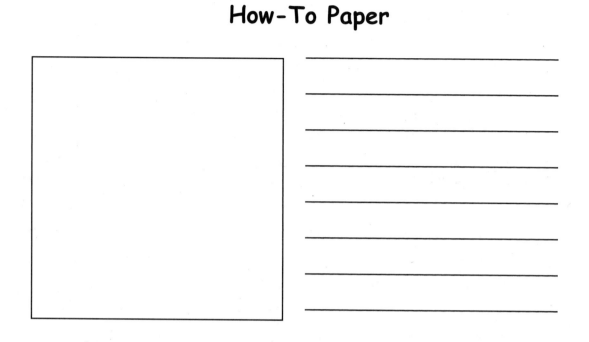

How-To Paper

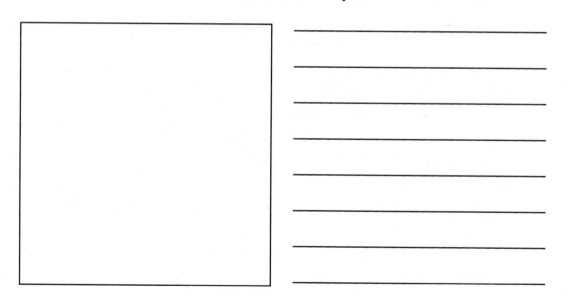

Materials Needed

Materials Needed

Appendix E

Picture Book Study Support Sheets

Picture Book Publishing Support Sheet

Growing writers help their readers understand and enjoy by:

1. Checking to see if the writing and illustrations are in the correct order

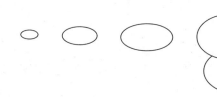

"Hmmm . . . let's see . . . page 1, illustration that goes with page 1, page 2, page 6 . . . Wait a minute! Page 6 doesn't go here!"

2. Rereading the piece for meaning and mechanics (editing checklist work) and then having a friend reread the piece for meaning and mechanics

"Oops! I forgot a word in this sentence! Let me fix that!" "Oh, I know that the first letter of every sentence begins with a capital letter! Let me check that."

3. Possibly adding words or illustrations that will better support the reader's understanding of the genre

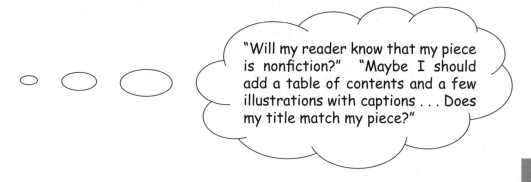

"Will my reader know that my piece is nonfiction?" "Maybe I should add a table of contents and a few illustrations with captions . . . Does my title match my piece?"

ABOUT THE AUTHOR

_____

_____

_____

_____

Photo of Author
Goes Here

_____

_____

_____

_____

_____

_____

_____

_____

Picture Book Paper

Children's Books

Anna's Table by Eve Bunting. 2003. Chanhassen, MN: NorthWord Press.

Antarctic Antics: A Book of Penguin Poems by Judy Sierra. 1998. San Diego, CA: Harcourt Brace.

Are You a Butterfly? by Judy Allen and Tudor Humphries. 2000. New York: Kingfisher.

Atlantic by G. Brian Karas. 2002. New York: Putnam.

Bat Loves the Night by Nicola Davies. 2001. Cambridge, MA: Candlewick.

Beast Feast: Poems and Paintings by Douglas Florian. 1994. San Diego, CA: Harcourt Brace.

Beekeepers by Linda Oatman High. 1998. Honesdale, PA: Boyds Mills Press.

Being Friends by Karen Beaumont. 2002. New York: Dial.

Black Cat by Christopher Myers. 1999. New York: Scholastic.

A Box of Friends by Pam Munoz Ryan. 2002. Columbus, OH: Gingham Dog Press.

The Burger and the Hot Dog by Jim Aylesworth. 2001. New York: Atheneum.

Chickerella by Mary Jane and Herm Auch. 2005. New York: Holiday House.

City Kids: Poems by Patricia Hubbell. 2001. New York: Marshall Cavendish.

Coin Magic by Cathy French. 2002. Pelham, NY: Benchmark.

Country Kid, City Kid by Julie Cummins. 2002. New York: Henry Holt.

Courage by Bernard Waber. 2002. New York: Walter Lorraine.

Diary of a Worm by Doreen Cronin. 2003. New York: Joanna Cotler Books.

Dirty Laundry Pile: Poems in Different Voices by Paul Janeczko. 2001. New York: HarperCollins.

Do the Lolly Trick by Sarah Fleming. 2000. Cambridge, UK: Cambridge University Press.

Do You Know What I'll Do? by Charlotte Zolotow. 2000. New York: HarperCollins.

Duckling by Lisa Magloff. 2003. New York: DK Publishing.

Earthworms by Lola M. Schaefer. 2002. Chicago: Heinemann Library.

Faces Only a Mother Could Love by Jennifer Owings Dewey. Honesdale, PA: Boyds Mills.

Fed Up by Rex Barron. 2000. New York: Putnam.

Flicker Flash by Joan Bransfield Graham. 1999. Boston: Houghton Mifflin.

Food Fight: Poets Join the Fight Against Hunger with Poems About Their Favorite Foods by Michael J. Rosen. 1996. San Diego: Harcourt Brace.

Get Red: An Adventure in Color by Tony Porto. 2002. Boston: Little, Brown.

Good Night, Pillow Fight by Sally Cook. 2004. New York: Joanna Cotler Books.

Grandpa's Soup by Eiko Kadono. 1999. Grand Rapids, MI: Eerdmans.

Have You Ever Done That? by Julie Larios. 2001. Asheville, NC: Front Street.

Hooray for Feet! by Susan Pearson. 2005. Maplewood, NJ: Blue Apple Books.

Hooray for You: A Celebration of "You-ness" by Marianne Richmond. 2001. Minneapolis, MN: Waldman House.

Hooway for Wodney Wat by Helen Lester. 1999. Boston: Houghton Mifflin.

Hottest, Coldest, Highest, Deepest by Steve Jenkins. 1998. Boston: Houghton Mifflin.

How to Be a Baby—By Me, The Big Sister by Sally Lloyd-Jones and Sue Heap. 2007. New York: Schwartz & Wade.

How to Tell Time: A Step-by-Step Guide for Kids and Their Grown-Ups by the editors of Klutz. 2005. Palo Alto, CA: Klutz.

I Am an Artist by Pat Lowery Collins. 1994. Brookfield, CT: Millbrook.

I Want to Be by Thylias Moss. 1993. New York: Dial.

Ice Bear: In the Steps of the Polar Bear by Nicola Davies. 2005. Cambridge, MA: Candlewick.

Imagine by Alison Lester. 1993. New York: Houghton Mifflin.

Imagine by Bart Vivian. 1994. Hillsboro, OR: Beyond Words.

The Incredible Book Eating Boy by Oliver Jeffers. 2007. New York: Philomel.

It's a Dog's New York by Susan Roth. 2001. Washington, DC: National Geographic.

It's a Frog's Life by Steve Parker. 1999. Pleasantville, NY: Reader's Digest.

It's an Ant's Life by Steve Parker. 1999. Pleasantville, NY: Reader's Digest.

It's Going to Be Perfect by Nancy Carlson. 1998. New York: Viking.

January Rides the Wind: A Book of Months by Charlotte F. Otten. 1997. New York: Lothrop, Lee & Shepard.

Jellyfish by Lola M. Schaefer. 2002. Chicago: Heinemann Library.

Leeches by Lola M. Schaefer. 2002. Chicago: Heinemann Library.

Lilly's Purple Plastic Purse by Kevin Henkes. 1996 . New York: Greenwillow Books.

Loki and Alex: The Adventures of a Dog and His Best Friend by Charles Smith. 2001. New York: Dutton.

Look to the North: A Wolf Pup Diary by Jean Craighead George. 1997. New York: HarperCollins.

Low Song by Eve Merriam. 2001. New York: Margaret K. McElderry.

Make a Banana Treat by Gill Budgell. 2000. Cambridge, UK: Cambridge University Press.

Make a Bird Feeder by Cathy French. Pelham, NY: Benchmark. 2002.

Make a Paper Hat by Sarah Fleming. 2000. Cambridge, UK: Cambridge University Press.

Make Colors by Gill Budgell. 2000. Cambridge, UK: Cambridge University Press.

Making a Bug Habitat by Natalie Lunis. 2002. Pelham, NY: Benchmark.

Making a Weather Station by Natalie Lunis. 2002. Pelham, NY: Benchmark.

Making Ice Cream by Natalie Lunis. 2002. Pelham, NY: Benchmark.

Mathematickles! by Betsy Franco. 2003. New York: Margaret K. McElderry.

My Big Sister by Valorie Fisher. 2003. New York: Atheneum.

My Big Sister by Valorie Fisher. 2003. New York: Atheneum.

My Brother by Anthony Browne. 2007. New York: Farrar, Straus and Giroux.

My Dad by Anthony Browne. 2000. New York: Farrar, Straus and Giroux.

My Map Book by Sara Fanelli. 1995. New York: HarperCollins.

My New York by Kathy Jakobson. 2003. New York: Little, Brown.

Newts by Lola M. Schaefer. 2002. Chicago: Heinemann Library.

Ordinary Things: Poems for a Walk in the Early Spring by Ralph Fletcher. 1997. New York: Atheneum.

Outside the Lines: Poetry at Play by Brad Burg. 2002. New York: Putnam.

Penguins Are Waterbirds by Sharon Taberski. 2002. New York: Mondo.

The Puddle Pail by Eliza Kleven. 2007. New York: Penguin.

Red Lace, Yellow Lace: Learn to Tie Your Shoes by Mike Casey. 1996. Hauppauge, NY: Barron's Educational Series.

Reptiles: A Close-Up Look at Our Cold Blooded Cousins by Sue Malyan. New York: DK.

Scarecrow by Cynthia Rylant. 2001. San Diego, CA: Voyager Books.

Scaredy Squirrel by Mélanie Watt. 2006. Tonawanda, NY: Kids Can Press.

Scaredy Squirrel Makes a Friend by Mélanie Watt. 2007. Tonawanda, NY: Kids Can Press.

Sea Anemones by Lola M. Schaefer. 2002. Chicago: Heinemann Library.

Serendipity by Tobi Tobias. 2000. New York: Simon and Schuster.

Shoe Magic by Nikki Grimes. 1990. New York: Scholastic.

Silver Seeds: A Book of Nature Poems by Paul Paolilli. 2001. New York: Viking.

Small Talk: A Book of Short Poems by Lee Bennett Hopkins. 1995. San Diego, CA: Harcourt Brace.

Some Things Are Scary by Florence Parry Heide. 2000. Cambridge, MA: Candlewick.

Stone Bench in an Empty Park by Paul Janeczko. 2000. New York: Orchard Books.

The Story of Grump and Pout! by Jamie McEwan. 1988. New York: Crown.

The Sunsets of Miss Olivia Wiggins by Lester Laminack. 1998. Atlanta, GA: Peachtree.

Super Snacks: Step by Step by Bobbie Kalman. 2003. New York: Crabtree.

Sweet, Sweet Memory by Jacqueline Woodson. 2000. New York: Hyperion.

Swing Around the Sun: Poems by Barbara Juster-Esbensen. 2003. Minneapolis, MN: Carolrhoda Books.

That Makes Me Mad! by Steven Kroll. 2002. New York: SeaStar Books.

Today I Feel Silly and Other Moods That Make My Day by Jamie Lee Curtis. 1998. New York: HarperCollins.

Treasures of the Heart by Alice Ann Miller. 2003. Chelsea, MI: Sleeping Bear Press.

Try This by Monica Hughes. 2000. Orlando, FL: Rigby.

Two Eggs Please by Sarah Weeks. 2003. New York: Atheneum.

The Undone Fairy Tale by Ian Lendler. 2005. New York: Simon and Schuster.

Water Planet by Ralph Fletcher. 1991. Paramus, NJ: Arrowhead Books.

The Way I Feel by Janan Cain. 2000. Seattle, WA: Parenting Press.

A Weekend with Wendell by Kevin Henkes. 1986. New York: Greenwillow Books.

Wemberly Worried by Kevin Henkes. 2000. New York: Greenwillow Books.

What Do You Do When Something Wants to Eat You? by Steve Jenkins. 1997. Boston: Houghton Mifflin.

What Do You Do With a Tail Like This? by Steve Jenkins. 2003. Boston: Houghton Mifflin.

What If?: Just Wondering Poems by Joy Hulme. 1993. Honesdale, PA: Boyds Mills.

What Makes Me Happy? by Catherine and Laurence Anholt. 1996. Cambridge, MA: Candlewick.

What's Up, What's Down by Lola M. Schaefer. 2002. New York: Greenwillow Books.

When Riddles Come Rumbling: Poems to Ponder by Rebecca Kai Dotlich. 2001. Honesdale, PA: Boyds Mills.

When Sophie Gets Angry—Really, Really Angry by Molly Bang. 1999. New York: Blue Sky Press.

Who Is the World For? by Tom Pow. 2000. Cambridge, MA: Candlewick.

Whoever You Are by Mem Fox. 1997. San Diego, CA: Harcourt Brace.

Why Does Lightning Strike?: Questions Children Ask About the Weather by Terry Martin. 2006. New York: DK Publishing.

Wilfred Gordon McDonald Partridge by Mem Fox. 1989. La Jolla, CA: Kane/Miller.

Wolves by Emily Gravett. 2006. New York: Simon and Schuster.

You Read to Me and I'll Read to You: Very Short Stories to Read Together by Mary Ann Hoberman. 2001. New York: Little, Brown.

Series

Meet the Author series. New York: Scholastic.

I Can Draw series. DK Publishing.

How-To series. Benchmark Education.

Watch Me Grow series. DK Publishing.

Look Closer series. DK Publishing.

See How They Grow series. Lodestar Books.

Read and Learn series. Heinemann.

References

Allington, Richard L. 2002. "What I've Learned About Effective Reading Instruction from a Decade of Studying Exemplary Elementary Classroom Teachers." *Phi Delta Kappan* 83(10): 740–747.

Beck, Isabel L., Margaret G. McKeown, and Linda Kucan. 2002. *Bringing Words to Life: Robust Vocabulary Instruction*. New York: Guilford.

Calkins, Lucy. 1994. *The Art of Teaching Writing*. Portsmouth, NH: Heinemann.

Dressel, Paul. 1983. "Grades: One More Tilt at the Windmill." In *Bulletin*, ed. Arthur W. Chickering. Memphis State University Center for the Study of Higher Education.

Fletcher, Ralph, and JoAnn Portalupi. 2001. *Writing Workshop: The Essential Guide*. Portsmouth, NH: Heinemann.

Graves, Donald. 2003. *Writing: Teachers and Children at Work*. 20th anniversary ed. Portsmouth, NH: Heinemann.

Harwayne, Shelley. 2001. *Writing Through Childhood: Rethinking Process and Product*. Portsmouth, NH: Heinemann.

Heard, Georgia. 1998. *Awakening the Heart: Exploring Poetry in Elementary and Middle School*. Portsmouth, NH: Heinemann.

Gambrell, Linda B., Lesley Mandell Morrow, and Michael Pressley, eds. 2007. *Best Practices in Literacy Instruction*. 3rd ed. New York: Guilford.

Jensen, Eric. 2003. *Environments for Learning*. San Diego, CA: The Brain Store.

———. 1998. *Teaching with the Brain in Mind*. Alexandria, VA: Association for Supervision and Curriculum Design.

Johnston, Peter. 2004. *Choice Words: How Our Language Affects Children's Learning.* Portland, ME: Stenhouse.

King, Stephen. 2000. *On Writing: A Memoir of the Craft.* New York: Simon and Schuster.

Kristo, Janice V., and Rosemary A. Bamford. 2004. *Nonfiction in Focus: A Comprehensive Framework for Helping Students Become Independent Readers and Writers of Nonfiction, K–6.* New York: Scholastic.

Lee, Harper. 1999. *To Kill a Mockingbird.* 40th anniversary ed. New York: HarperCollins.

Portalupi, JoAnn, and Ralph Fletcher. 2001. *Nonfiction Craft Lessons: Teaching Information Writing K–8.* Portland, ME: Stenhouse.

Ray, Katie Wood, and Lisa Cleaveland. 2004. *About the Authors: Writing Workshop with Our Youngest Writers.* Portsmouth, NH: Heinemann.

Ray, Katie Wood, and Lester Laminack. 2001. *The Writing Workshop: Working Through the Hard Parts (And They're All Hard Parts).* Urbana, IL: National Council of Teachers of English.

Routman, Regie. 2005. *Writing Essentials: Raising Expectations and Results While Simplifying Teaching.* Portsmouth, NH: Heinemann.

Stead, Tony. 2001. *Is That a Fact? Teaching Nonfiction Writing K–3.* Portland, ME: Stenhouse.

Taberski, Sharon. 2000. *On Solid Ground: Strategies for Teaching Reading K–3.* Portsmouth, NH: Heinemann.

Taberski, Sharon. 2002. Workshop presentation at the District 2 Principal's Conference. New York City. Dec. 11.

Index